"…WITHOUT PROBATION, PAROLE, OR SUSPENSION OF SENTENCE"

My First Year of Incarceration

SHERRAL D. KAHEY

Order this book online at www.trafford.com
or email orders@trafford.com

Most Trafford titles are also available at major online book retailers.

Printed in the United States of America.

ISBN: 978-1-4669-5456-4 (sc)
ISBN: 978-1-4669-5455-7 (e)

Trafford rev. 09/06/2012

 www.trafford.com

North America & international
toll-free: 1 888 232 4444 (USA & Canada)
phone: 250 383 6864 ♦ fax: 812 355 4082

FOREWORD

L ouisiana imprisons more people than any nation in the world. Louisiana imprisons more of its residents than any other state in the United States.

As the incarceration rate doubled in the last two decades, local sheriffs began to build prisons to house state offenders to help accommodate the growing prison population. It is interesting to note that correction jobs and local economies rely upon the daily state rate of $24.39 per day that it pays sheriffs and local *for profit* prisons to house offenders. The average daily price tag for an inmate in a state prison is $55.00 per day. The political pressure to keep beds full is a contributing factor to Louisiana's world-leading incarceration rate.[1]

There are a number of reasons for prisons—punishment, deterrence, public safety, and rehabilitation. With dwindling resources at the State level, programs in state prisons are on the decline. Prisons run by local sheriff's offices are only able to offer limited programs. There is no financial incentive for private *for profit* prisons to offer programs.

In Louisiana, a life sentence is a sentence where the offender will serve their natural life in the custody of the Louisiana Department of Corrections. If the district attorney seeks a capital verdict, the offender in a first degree murder case shall be punished by death or life imprisonment at hard labor without benefit of parole, probation,

---

[1]   The Times Picayune, May 13, 2012.

or suspension of sentence. The penalty for a second degree murder conviction is life imprisonment at hard labor without benefit of parole, probation, or suspension of sentence.

One Friday in October 2002 I was asked to speak at a *Friends and Family Day* banquet for women who were serving life sentences at the Louisiana Correctional Institute for Women. The theme was "There Can Be Miracles If You Believe". I had some hesitancy with accepting the invitation, as I was not sure if I would be able to come up with a message that would connect with women offenders who were destined to die in prison, without the intervention of a miracle.

My mother, Avis Baker-White, came with me to LCIW that night. As we entered the multi-purpose room, my eyes surveyed the audience and I wondered when the officials were going to bring in the offenders. As I mingled with the persons in the audience, I realized that the offenders were already there. A *light bulb* clicked in my head when I realized that the offenders looked like me, my mother, my sister or my daughter.

When it was my opportunity to speak, I brought greetings from my father, who had worked as a pharmacist at LCIW for seven or eight years. The *Prayer of Jabez* was popular during that time and I used its tenets as part of my motivational message.

When I pulled together the outline of my speech, I felt inadequate. I remember thinking that there was nothing that I could possibly say that could touch women who were serving life sentences. Even though my speech was well received, I remember feeling guilty after I spoke to the women that night, because they had such great faith. I left feeling that I had received more from the women that night than I gave.

After the speech, I was somewhat conflicted. I thought that If I had certain stereotypical prejudices about offenders, then perhaps the public did also. While I was on the dais, I leaned over to Warden Johnnie A. Jones and asked if he would consent to me facilitating an educational program with women offenders in area schools. That night the Warden gave his blessing to the concept and the first educational tour began in 2003.

I received a call from my Aunt Vera the Monday following the speech. She said that three newspapers had collected in my father's yard and that she had not seen him in a couple of days. When I entered his home, I knew what I would find. I found my father's lifeless body. I believe that my father died the day that I was speaking to the women at LCIW.

I do not believe in coincidences. Two days after finding my father's body, I received a letter from Sherral. In the letter she said that my father talked about me often while she assisted him in the pharmacy. She also said that he talked about how much he loved me. That disclosure really warmed my heart, because my father had never said that he loved me while he was alive. It is no way that Sherral could have known that my father was dead when she wrote the letter.

In 2003 I dedicated the educational tour to the memory of my father, Gilbert A. White. Since that time, I have gotten to know Sherral very well as she was one of the blue card holders (trustees) selected by LCIW to participate in the educational programs in area schools.

Trudy M. White, Judge
19tt Judicial District Court
State of Louisiana

INTRODUCTION

My primary reason for writing this book is to depict a realistic and accurate portrayal of what life is really like behind the bars in a women's penal facility. Incarceration is not what the media and big screen portray. Life behind bars is much like life is society, with the obvious exceptions. There is good and bad, right and wrong in both worlds. Not all women sentenced to penal facilities deserve the stringent sentences handed down to them. Conversely, not all the people who have the privilege to walk "freely" in society are deserving of that privilege.

The secondary reason for writing this book is to find personal healing, to make sense of the situations and to hopefully help someone else along the way. Everything happens for a reason and good comes from every situation. I needed to make sense of the time that I was away from my loved one. I needed to isolate the good from this dreadful experience and discord the bad. My children and I were separated from each other in 1980. In 2009, I walked out of LCIW as a free woman. You do the math on the time I was away from my children. It is staggering yet real.

I would like for readers of this book to enjoy the book, but not at the expense of educating and enlightening readers about the cold, hard realities of female incarceration. People who are convicted of crimes are criminals; however all criminals are not bad people. Some great people have had the misfortune of being incarcerated, yet had the tenacity to make a positive message from their negative mess.

Sherral D. Kahey

Dedicated to the Lifers, past, present and future,
of the Louisiana Correctional Institute for Women

THE BEGINNING OF THE END

"Sherral Kahey, stand to your feet," I acquiesced, the judge continued, "you have been found guilty by this court of the charge of Principle to Second Degree Murder in the death of one Curtiss Baldwell. It is my duty to sentence you to life in prison at hard labor to be served without the benefit of probation, parole, or suspension of the sentence. You are to begin serving this sentence immediately."

The day was August 2, 1982. It was a cold atmosphere inside that courtroom on a hot, sticky, humid August morning in northern Louisiana. There it ended; there it began. The judge had taken my life from me, in those few seconds; with those harsh words. That day was the end of my freedom, the beginning of life behind bars, without probation, life without a parole date, and life without the benefit of having my sentence suspended. L-I-F-E! I was ending a life I had lived for thirty-three years. I was beginning a life in prison that, according to the judge, would be my final resting place. I was a convicted felon beginning a life inside an unknown, unfriendly and disdainful world that, by all intents and purposes, would be my "home" for the duration of my time on earth. That was a solemn, sobering thought.

Standing tall at five feet, eight inches, shoulders squared, chin up, defiantly refusing to show the judge and the audience any signs of emotion, I turned to view my family. My only sister, Robin, stood. She was holding my four-month-old baby, Asia. I had only spent two months of Asia's life with her. Robin started walking toward me. With each step Robin made in my direction, a single tear dropped from her eyes, she took a step, she dropped a tear, she took another step; she dropped another tear. Time froze for that instant, like in the movies when everything is going in slow motion then suddenly stops. No one moved except for my sister. No one said a word. It appeared as if everyone was holding his or her breath; frozen in time. About five feet from my sister's destination, a husky, tobacco-mouthed, potbelly, and red-faced bailiff stepped between us.

"Please, Mister, let my sister hold her baby one last time," my sister petitioned. The tears had not stopped even though her procession had.

"Can't do that, Ma'am," he denied her request, coldly. "Court is still in session, Ma'am and you have to take a seat or you will be held in contempt of court. The Judge is not finished."

That was ironic, what more could he say? He had ended my life, so what was left, I thought to myself. My sister was not giving up so easily. She reiterated her request.

"My God, Sir, let her hold and kiss her baby. This will be the last time she can do it!" my sister beseeched. She was crying openly now. My heart bled for her. I wanted to break down at that moment and join her in her outpouring. Yet, my pride would not allow me the luxury of showing emotions. I knew "they" wanted to see me broken, desperate, and humbled by the knowledge that I was going to prison. No, it just was not happening, not here, not now.

It wasn't so much that I was being rebellious; I just knew that this whole trial and the process was a farce, I was not guilty of the charge. I knew that and I also knew that the judge, the District Attorney the Indigent Defender, and everyone who looked at the case knew that this was a travesty of justice. While my sister wailed, I stood there watching her in utter stillness.

"Ma'am, you have to take a seat," this man was the epitome of heartlessness. Robin plopped into the nearest seat, her tears and soft sobs had now turned to a whispered prayer. I could hear the phonetics hiss of the "s" words as she conversed with the God that she believed, relied on, trusted in and depended on. Robin had made the plea to the court, now she was taking the plea to the God she wanted to intervene in this situation on her behalf.

The judge appeared undaunted by this brief exchange. A man in his 60s, Judge Robert Lee Beckett, had a head full of shiny silver hair, combed to the back. He had pale blue eyes that seemed to look through you, a look that actually chilled me to my bones. His white face seemed pale even more so against the color of the proverbial black robe.

Judge Beckett continued his spiel, "You will be remanded to the department of corrections where you will serve out your sentence at hard labor for the rest of your natural life." That was the rest of it. He added insult to injury. He told me of my life and my death.

Hard labor? Was that a play on words? I had labored hard to bring five lives into this world. Now, this mere man was taking my life away from me. My thoughts drifted to my other four offspring's: Monet, 14; Jaheim, 9; Victor, 4; and Ethiopia, 2 years old. My babies would grow up without a mother. My babies were sentenced to a life without a mother. Did the judge care? Should he care? Do my babies understand what was happening? Did they realize the judge's words were also sentencing them?

"Bailiff," the judge ordered, "remove the prisoner from the courtroom."

"Your Honor, Sir", my sister spoke, "can Sherral just hold and kiss her little baby girl and her other children for the last time, please." The judge let his eyes roll over my sister as if she were the filth of the earth. He turned to the bailiff and said, "Bailiff, remove the prisoner!"

"Oh Judge, please have mercy on my sister! Please, don't take her away from me, from us!" Shamelessly, my sister cried before God and everyone in sight.

As the bailiff handcuffed me, I gazed into my sister's teary eyes and tear-stained face and said, "It's okay, it'll be alright". Why did I say those words in the face of the words I had just heard spoken by the judge? Everything was wrong. The "kangaroo" bench trial that had just convicted me was wrong. The Indigent Defender that only had four weeks to prepare for my trial was wrong. The fact that I was forced to accept an indigent defender was wrong. The life sentence I received was wrong. The Caucasian judge was wrong, the indifferent bailiff was wrong. There was no right in these wrongs, so what was I thinking? What was I talking about, saying, *"It is alright"*? What was I doing here?

"It's not right, Cookie," my sister hissed at me. She called me by the nickname that my great-grandmother had given me at birth. Lying in a dresser drawer in a makeshift bed cushioned with a feather tick pillow, Big Mama said I looked like a gingerbread cookie; thus the birth of the name that I was never able to shake.

"What's right about you spending the rest of your life in prison, huh, tell me that! What's right about your children sitting over there," she pointed in my children's direction, "crying their hearts out and no one, not even you, seem to care!!"

What could I say? As of this day, August 2, 1982, I had no voice, no life, and no children. I had no family, friends, or any other relations as I had known before this dreadfully sorrowful moment in time. My life took a twisted turn toward "Hell".

All I could think about was how things had gotten this bad for me. I wasn't a bad person. All my life I believed that if I did good things for and to people, good things would come back to me. Conversely, if I did evil, evil would return to me. It wasn't a spiritual thing or even a religious thing. It was a fact of life, the cycle of life and the way things happened. I thought of something my great aunt told me when, at ten years old, my 28-year old mother had died of Leukemia. She was too young to die; I was too young to be motherless. Crying, I declared to Auntie, "It isn't fair". Auntie walked around the table and kneeled in front of me at the chair where I sat crying my heart's sad song. "Cookie, let me tell you something, life isn't fair. Who told you life was fair? The sooner you learn that the better off you'll be. Life will land you some cold, hard blows. You have to decide how to receive them. Are you gonna double over and give up, just crying and get beat up by life, or are you gonna absorb the blows and fight back? Cookie, you gotta meet life on its terms, roll with the punches, fall down, get knocked down, trip, stumble, land on your feet or git back up ready for the next blow, cause it's coming. Fight back and survive or throw the towel in and live life as a loser, a quitter, and that ain't no life at all." That was Auntie. She had a saying for every situation a person encountered. For a while, I really thought that Auntie was the writer of the Book of Proverbs in the Holy Bible. Later I learned that although she didn't write the book, she read it often because it was her favorite book in the Bible and she lived by the sage entries from Proverbs. She was a warrior. She was my role model. I loved her.

Life isn't fair. The unfairness of life had brought me to a penal facility where I had some life-changing and life-challenging lessons to learn. The biggest challenge for me was whether or not this education that I was about to receive would make me or break me.

In order to learn the lessons that were set before me; in order to take these lessons and come out of this situation better than I was when I entered, I needed to survive some hellish situations with my sanity intact.

My state of mind was totally dependent upon my outlook on life. I had been dealt a bitter hand. It was not fair, but the situation's unfairness did not negate the reality that I was here serving a life sentence which meant, according to the judicial system, that I entered the facility on two feet carrying a black bag. I would exit the facility on my back, lifeless and carried *in* a black body bag. That grim thought was enough to delivery me into the hands of insanity. I was bitter, no doubt. I was angry with myself for the chain of poor choices that led me to face this travesty. I was angry with Allah *(God)* for the free will He had afforded me to make the poor choices and for His allowing me to do so. I was angry with my Islamic husband who thought he was a god and chose to have several wives. I was angry with the judicial system that I thought would be blind and unbiased. The anger that I harbored would be my survival strategy or it would be my emotional and mental undoing. That choice was mine. The bottom-line was that I had to find a means to exist in this environment without losing my mind.

INTAKE: THE MADNESS BEGINS

The Louisiana Correctional Institute for Women (LCIW) looked like a college campus. The landscape appeared to be something from one of those classy garden magazines. Flowers and beautiful greenery adorned this warehouse of human beings. The grass was immaculately manicured and so green that it looked unreal. The sidewalks were made of cobblestone and were swept clean. The buildings looked freshly painted and the windows sparkled. The environment appeared clean and inviting. Yet I had the lingering suspicion that underneath the immaculately manicured shrubbery, the clean appearance, and flowery fragrance that emitted into the air this place was every bit the "hell" that I had envisioned.

The entrance to the facility was an iron gate that had the loudest buzzer I had ever heard. When the buzzer sounded the guard pushed the iron gate and escorted the inmates into the foyer of the entrance. Here was where we were relieved of our handcuffs and any other restraints that we were wearing. The guard behind the counter of this entrance asked the officer for our names and what parish had sent us. Sometimes the parish bus would bring the inmates. Other times the parish was responsible for delivering the inmates to the "big house" which is what it was called in the parish jails and prisons. The parish that had sentenced me had delivered me to what the judge said would be my final destination on this earth.

Across from where I stood there was a large room full of tables and chairs. Above the door as I glanced up I saw a plaque that said

"Visiting Room". So, this was where family and friends came to visit their loved ones who were incarcerated. The tables and chairs were cramped in this room making it appear crowded even in its empty state at present. I could imagine how crowded this room appeared when it was full of visitors and inmates. Some tables were long and rectangular others were short and square. The long tables had eight to ten chairs on either side while the short square tables had only four chairs. There was what appeared to be a school teacher's desk diagonally positioned in the entrance of the visiting area. This desk was old and battered; large and heavy-looking. There was a chair at this desk and another along the side of the desk. It did not take a rocket scientist to figure out that this was where the officer sat in order to observe the activities that took place in the visiting room.

At the far end of the room there was a long, wall-to-wall, three-tiered shelf. The shelves were full of crafts such as Afghans, stuffed pillows, canvas jewelry boxes, needlepoint work, and all sort of knit, sewing and crochet items. Some of the items were beautifully and meticulously crafted while other items look like items one's first grader would bring home. Some of the items were covered in clear plastic while other items were not. There were tiny pieces of paper on these items that I later discovered where the name of the female who made the item, her department of corrections (DOC) number, and the price of the item. It was apparent that the shelves were filled with crafts that the inmates had made with the hope of selling them to visitors.

There were six "new commits" in all. That is what we were called, "new commits". New commits were added to the prison population once a week on a Tuesday. I had all my worldly possessions in a black garbage bag given to me when I left the parish jail. We could not have any type of luggage and if what I had in the parish jail did not fit in that black bag, it had to be left behind. The new commits knew very little about each other, mainly basic information. There was an unspoken rule in prison; you do not ask certain questions such as: How much time you got" or "What is your charge?" If a person wanted to share this information, it was strictly up to her to do so without prompting, prodding, probing or picking.

No one told you this. There was no written rule for it; it was just a fact, a line that no one crossed. If someone did, that person was given a reputation of being "in yo' business" and, largely, avoided by the other offenders.

Our group included, besides me, **Carlas**, who was proud to say that she was a repeat offender several times over. Carlas was medium height, about 5' 5". She was chubby and she wore her hair in cornrows. She was medium brown-skinned and she had a set of beautiful teeth and eyes. Carlas seemed to be a confident female straight from the "ghetto". She boasted of growing up in the projects and streets of New Orleans. Her grammar was a form of broken English and French. She talked excessively. I wonder on more than one occasion whether or not her endless chatter had to do with nervousness. Actually, Carlas got on my nerves most of the time. There were times when I wanted to tell her to shut up! Carlas bragged about being the best shoplifter in New Orleans. My question was if she were such a great thief, why was she always getting caught? Carlas must have read my expression because she said, "I don't come to jail for shoplifting, I comes for doing drugs, you know, possession charges". That was Carlas, the veteran female offender.

Velma was what offenders called a "Main Liner". Main Liners did anything and everything to support their heroin habits. Velma was tall, skinny to the point of looking anorexic. She had pale pink skin that looked as if she needed some sun. Her blonde hair was cut short revealing a long, skinny neck full of ugly track marks. She was the only Caucasian in our group of six. You had to look at her to know she was Caucasian, because she acted, spoke, and carried herself as if either she were a black girl passing for white or she had spent a lot of time with Blacks. Velma had the remnants of a beautiful woman, probably before the heroin habit took control of her mind and body. She tried to maintain her appearance however the heroin had robbed her of her original beauty. Velma was a heroin-addicted prostitute from Lake Charles, Louisiana.

Brenda, who was from Alexandria, Louisiana, was reluctant to speak. One could tell from observing her body language that she had encountered and possibly endured abuse in one or more of its forms. In my analytical mind I decided that Brenda had been married to an abusive man. She wore a gold wedding band on the ring finger of her left hand. I also noticed that she fidgeted with the ring in what I thought was a nervous gesture. For certain Brenda had low self-esteem marked by her reticence to hold her head up or look into the eyes of those to whom she spoke. Brenda was pretty in a plain sort of way. She had smooth black skin, long auburn dyed hair, and a soft, quiet voice. Brenda was tall, about 5'10", and slender. Her eyes were light brown, but they were sad eyes. She appeared to be on the verge of crying all the time. One had to strain to hear what she said when she did speak. Because she seldom said anything, when she did speak, it was like the E.F Hutton commercial, "everyone listened". The first words I heard her speak were, "When do we get to use a phone?" We stared at her for a moment to see if she was going to burst into tears, although it appeared so, she did not. Brenda's question was one that was probably on all our minds. That question went unanswered for a short time.

Lucinda had embezzled money. She did not mind telling us about her charge. She declared her charge as if it really was not a crime as in killing someone. Lucinda was quiet and timid. She was Hispanic. Her skin was olive and her hair was jet black. Everything about her was just average. Lucinda was chubby, but not so much so that she looked fat. She was average in height, about 5'4". She appeared to be scared. I think she was in denial about her incarceration because she never referred to prison in the classic terms. She called it the "*campus*". Lucinda, who was from the New Orleans area did not like for people to say that she was from New Orleans. Whenever anyone said that she was from New Orleans, Lucinda quickly corrected them by saying that she was from "Algiers". Lucinda did not seem to want to be part of our group. She was aloft and guarded in her mannerism. We respected each other's space, not wanting to intrude or impose. Lucinda was an educated female, which was obvious when she spoke. She was also somewhat "stuck-up". It was as if she thought better of herself than she did any of us.

Lastly, there was **Josie** who was covered with tattoos and seemed not to want to say anything to anyone. She was short in statue, yet she possessed an aura of superiority. Josie was coal black and appeared to be proud of her darkness. She was always looking in the mirror that she carried around with her. Her features were African, white eyes; full, thick lips; wide nose. Josie had natural hair that she wore loose with a bandana circling the crown of her head. For some reason, I felt that she wanted to front the appearance of being a rough and tough character. In fact I thought that Josie may have been "gay", or as the prison called them, a "stud-broad'. However, underneath that hard exterior, she was a soft and sensitive individual. I actually wondered how she came to be incarcerated. She was the only one in our group that sparked that question in my mind. Although, I did not feel that I was typically viewed as a convict, I knew my situation, I was perplexed about Josie's.

Neophytes entering the women's penal facility were not called "fresh fish" or "fresh meat" by the other offenders as is so often characterized on the television and the "big screen. But now being incarcerated, I understood the idea behind the terms. The inmates eyed us down as if we were slaves on the trading block. That is, at least the way I felt as I was escorted from place to place. Offenders lined up along the compound sidewalks to have a look at us as we were being escorted to the intake area. I felt as if we were on display. It gave me an uneasy feeling as if I were being sized up for some reason currently unknown to me. I wanted to ask them what they were looking at. None of us had horns or a tail! However, we were scrutinized as if we were from another planet.

"Take your clothes off and hand them to me, one piece at a time," the officer spoke in a monotone that let me know she was a no non-sense person. Her uniform was navy blue double knit slacks and a short-sleeve navy shirt with red-trimmed piping down the outside of the pant legs and on the shirt sleeves. The brass name plate pinned to her shirt revealed her name, Sgt. Wicken", I was in a small room labeled "snake room."

"Yes Ma'am," I replied, After all, what else was there to say? I proceeded to comply with her order.

"Hurry up, I ain't got all day. I got five more of you convicts to look at," Sgt Wicken's tone was curt. I continued to undress as fast as I could and handed each garment to the officer. Finally, there I stood, as naked as I was when I came into the world. Sgt. Wicken looked over my body, as I stood in front of her feeling as naked and uncovered figuratively as I was literally.

"Now, turn your butt to me, bend over and touch your toes, then take your hands, spread open the cheeks of your butt and cough hard," Sgt. Wicken commanded me. I'd never heard orders like that before, but something told me I'd hear orders of that nature a lot more before it was over.

"AHUH ahuh!" I bent over and coughed as hard as I could, simply because I did not want to repeat this drill again. As I rose, I asked, "Was that okay"

"You tryin' to be smart, Convict!" Sgt. Wicken barked at me. She was angry. I was perplexed.

"Did I say something to upset you?" I asked, sincere in my concern. I felt that with what I had just endured, I should have been the one who was upset.

"Smart mouth convicts always upset me." Sgt Wicken said the word "*convict*" with sheer contempt. I wondered whether her distain for "convicts" had anything to do with her possibly having been victimized.

"Excuse me, Ma'am, I just wanted to get it right the first time, that's all", I tried my best to patch the situation.

"You better know one thing about me, if you hadda did it wrong, I'd a-told you so, now shut up talking to me and get your clothes on and git outta here and send the next one in to me. After I dressed, I silently headed toward the exit door, glad to be over this phase of the intake process, then:

"Oh hell no! You almost made me forget my job, you talk too much, git your Chatter-box, ass back over here", Sgt. Wicken seemed irritated.

"Do I have to undress again?" I asked.

"Git over here like I said, you ask too many questions." I walked over to the sergeant praying that she wouldn't ask or order me to strip naked once again.

"Come here. Let me check your other cavities." stated Sgt. Wicken.

"No need for that, I don't have any cavities. I had them filled years ago. I take care of my teeth and so I don't have any cavities." I was pleased to report my excellent hygiene report. In fact, I was very much proud of my pearly white teeth. People often told me that my teeth and my smile were my best features.

"Oh yeah, "Convict" you in the right place to get broke. You a smart-ass nigga." The "N" word sounded odd emanating from Sgt. Wicken since she was about three shades darker than I. She continued, "I see already we got a problem on our hands, but we knows how to deal with cons like you."

I stood there silently. She kept talking, "Open your f-ing mouth 'fore I put my fist in it." This officer radiated such venom, such aggression, and such a foul-mouth. Was she the rule or the exception? Were all the penal officers borderline illiterate bullies who attempted to intimidate and crush the underdog-"cons"? Was Sgt. Wicken threatening me in an attempt to put fear in me? Was I going to have to defend myself against this officer? Would I be beaten within an inch of my life by this officer and her comrades? I was terrified. I didn't know what I had said that sent this person into a violent verbal frenzy. I felt intimidated true enough, but I was not going to give Officer Wicken the satisfaction of knowing that she had succeeded in putting fear into my heart.

I slowly walked back to the officer, not at all clear, about what was going to happen to me once I reached her. I stopped directly in front of her, my knees shaking and my heart beating so fast that I thought that I may have been threatening a heart attack. I stood toe-to-toe with Sgt. Wicken, eye-to-eye to her. I defiantly opened my mouth waiting for her fist to enter and several of my teeth to be destroyed. I braced for the fist that I knew would relieve me of my two beautiful white front teeth.

"Open your mouth wide" the officer demanded. I did. Sgt. Wicken stuck her gloved finger in my mouth and circled it around inside. I thought about biting her finger off but of course thought better of it. "Don't you bite me either," she said, verbalizing my thought. She removed her finger from my mouth.

"Now, turn your head so I can see inside your ears", she commanded.

Feeling like a child, I complied, sheepishly. With the same, now wet, gloved hand, the officer yanked my ear closer to her face. It hurt, I flinched and Officer Wicken snickered. She probed inside my ears one at a time. I winced; the damp gloved hand that touched my ears felt clammy. Again, I heard this officer snicker at her antics. She took perverted pleasure in tormenting me.

Sgt. Wicken was checking my cavities. The two main cavities had been checked while I was naked and bent over; my nostrils, ears, and mouth constituted the other cavities totaling seven.

The penal system has a language all its own; a language within a language. I was entering an educational system unlike any other. There were no degrees to earn here. This education was one of survival of the strongest. This education included the ins and outs; the ups and downs; the do's and don'ts of the system. There were no books to study. I had to study the elements that I had to interact with—guards and female offenders.

Outside the shake room, curious eyes searched my face for any sign of what to expect or what I had gone through. I would not give them that satisfaction. They would have to wait their turn to see experience what was behind the door. To add to their apprehension, my clothes were in total disarray.

"What happened to you in there?" someone asked, I didn't recognize the voice, since I had not been among them long enough to distinguish voices.

"What happened to you?"

"I got raped! That's what happened to me." I answered.

"No, you didn't," Lucinda's statement sounded more like a question than a statement.

"Did you for real, get raped?" inquired Velma, who seemed terrified at that thought. I felt sorry for her so I clarified my statement.

"No, I didn't get raped literally, but figuratively, yes. I had to take off all my clothes while the officer watched me from head to toe and further. With her eyes, or her hands, she looked in or at every part of my body."

"Next Convict get in here, I ain't got all day. Com'moan in here." Sgt Wicken's tone was what ended my put-on. One-by-one each of the others went into the small shake room and exited a little less self-possessed.

An officer whose name badge informed me that her name was Sgt. P. Jones, came to escort us to a room where the clothes and other items we brought with us were sprawled all over the floor in six different piles.

"Find your belongings and stand next to'em", she said calmly. This officer was nicer and more patient than the first one. "I gotta itemize your property. I can tell you right now, you won't be able to keep a lot of this stuff. Please don't waste my time asking me questions, the sooner we get this over with, the sooner you'll have this behind you."

"Yeah, yes, Yes Ma'am, Okay, uh-huh, Yep, fuh-sho", came our varied unison replies.

"Good, we understand each other. Let us get busy, then," instructed Sgt. Moore. Throughout the remainder of the morning, we sorted through our clothes and trashed some of the few items we were allowed to bring that were some of our most personal and intimate things: pictures, clothing items, letters, and memories of a time and place long since lost to us. Part of each of us died that day with each memory that we had to discard.

This experience was yet another lesson, property had to be itemized and counted. Items over the specified amount were either mailed to family if you had the postage stamps to do so, or they were destroyed. I remarked to myself, *"Earlier, we had been stripped physically, now we are being stripped, emotionally. What was next? Driving us insane? Was that the mental stripping? To strip us of our sanity?* Velma broke the silence ending my mental conversation. "Girls, I had to get rid of my new panties 'cause they were bikinis."

"I had to get rid of my panties 'cause I had too many." complained Brenda. "Can you believe these people only want you to have seven pair of panties? Disgusting!" she concluded.

"Well, they should have let you give your extra panties to me," commented Carlas, "all I got is the ones I'm wearing now." That, to me, was really disgusting!

"As many times as you've been through this system, you should have known what you could and could not have, Carlas. Damn!" Brenda said, sounding irritated.

Look, Smarty, I know what I could and could not have, that don't mean I could get it. Don't nobody do nothing for me when I'm in jail." Carlas said, defending herself. "Anyway," she continued, "rules change around here every day. Don't nothing stay the same."

"COUNT TIME! COUNT TIME! ALL RESIDENTS STAND QUIETLY BY YOUR BED, PROPERLY ATTIRED, NO EXCESSIVE MOVEMMENT, NO TALKING, NO CHEWING GUM AND STAND QUIETLY UNTIL THE OFFICER CALLS COUNT CLEARED. IT IS NOW COUNT TIME IN ALL AREAS". This was the call as the officer entered the door of the infirmary. It startled me, and a few others. Of course, our friend Carlas, was not effected in the least.

"Y'all stand by your beds," she instructed us. We did as we were told.

"Carlas, I know you ain't talking during my count!" said the officer who had entered and made the announcement.

"No, ma'am, Miss Evans, I was jest telling them to stand up." Carlas informed the officer.

"Then that constitutes talking, in my book," replied the officer, "so you better shut up or git wrote up!"

Counting is the method for keeping account for the prisoners. There are about six counts each day beginning at 4:30 a.m. We had missed the first counts because of our intake process. After the count was cleared, we resumed our previous conversation.

"How long were you out?" I asked.

"What, this time?" she asked, "Yeah, well this time, here, this time, I mean I, I uh I stayed out a year," Carlas seemed ashamed for the first time. I was actually relieved to see that there was a feeling of shame in Carlas. There was hope for her, yet.

"So, you think that in a year, the itemized property list has changed?" Lucinda asked.

Sgt. Ruffin answered this time, "The Standardized Itemized List has not changed in the last seven years." All eyes went to Carlas for a rebuttal.

"I can't' 'member all that stuff," was her only response.

"For the first time since my conviction and sentencing, I feel like I am really in prison," said Lucinda, sadly. We all nodded our agreement and were silent, lost in our own thoughts and memories for a time. For me, as well, this was the first time I felt like a criminal. My mind and my body had been violated. My privacy had been violated. My property had been violated. I had to discard possessions that had sentimental value to no one, except me. There was no two ways about it, we were told to destroy small pieces of our life and we did. It was suicide. There was no sympathy, no compassion or empathy. No matter what you said, if the officer said, "trash it", we had to trash it.

"Hey Sherral", Velma whispered, "look," Velma was clutching something in her hand.

She leaned close to my ear and whispered, "I snuck my little girl's picture while the officer was counting my socks." Velma actually seemed excited about her "steal".

Velma clutched a tattered photo of a beautiful "mixed" child who looked like a black version of Velma. The child, a girl, appeared to be about three years old.

"She blowin' out her birthday candles, see? It's three of 'em".

"Oh, Velma, she is beautiful!" I exhorted Velma who was staring at the photo as if it were the first time she had seen it. Momentarily, she was lost in thought.

"Yeah, Sherral, she is", Velma held the picture closed to her eyes, as if to get a better look.

"She look just like her daddy, well except for the color, 'cause her daddy is coal black."

"No, Velma, I think she looks like you." I observed.

"Naw, she is her daddy's baby for sho'. She gonna be dark like him, too." Velma spoke those words as if they were a command or a wish. She wanted this baby to be black and to show it.

"Velma, why is this picture so special to you?" I asked wanting to know.

"Glad you asked, Sherral, Velma began, "well, you see me in that picture?" I shook my head in answer to her question.

"Well, you see, on this birthday, it was the first time since she been born that I was sober. My mama let me come to her party and that was the first time I seen her since she was born." Velma's countenance revealed a glimpse of both pride and humiliation.

"What do you mean, "Lucinda asked, puzzled, "didn't you see her in the hospital when you had her?"

"Lucinda, I didn't have her in the hospital. I had her at a shootin' gallery." Velma spoke those words so low and softly that I had to strain to hear her.

"A what?" I asked. It wasn't that I didn't hear what she said, I didn't understand what she meant by what she said.

Brenda spoke this time, "A shootin' gallery is an old abandoned house or apartment where heroin addicts go to shoo up they dope."

Velma said, "Yep, I was so strung out on that shit, I didn't even know I was in labor." Velma hung her head in shame and remorse. I was glad to see that slight show of emotion.

A moment passed before she said another word. Then, "My baby was born with a habit," Velma said, crying. I felt sorry for her. She continued the account of her baby girl's birth. "Somebody called my mama and she came to the "gallery" and took us to the hospital. I don't remember any of that. I'm just repeating what my mama told me about it. Ain't that pitiful, can't even remember the birth of my own-self's baby." She paused and I thought she had ended her dialogue.

"I gave mama custody of the baby", Velma continued, "but Rashad would not give my mama full custody cause he wanted the baby, but he didn't have no job or no place to stay." Velma needed to get this off her chest so we let her talk. She continued, "He cared mo'bout the baby than I did. Hell, he cared mo' 'bout the baby than he cared 'bout me. He even quit doing heroin, and he done it cold turkey! When I wouldn't leave the drugs alone, he up and left me just like that." She snapped her fingers.

I knew a little about what "cold turkey" was because my first husband was a junkie strung out on herion. Cold turkey was when a junkie withdrew from drugs in order to kick the habit. Cold turkey was a long, slow, painful process that was not a pretty sight to witness. The person would get physically ill, vomit, cry; the body would tremble from wanting and craving the drug. The person would have symptoms of a cold or even the flu. I watched my husband try going cold turkey once and believe me, once was enough for me. He did not succeed and went back to shooting heroin with an even greater fervor.

I thought to myself, sadly, "I wasn't a drug user, I loved my children and only wanted the best, or what I thought was best for them. I had completely given myself to the upbringing of my children. What had happened? What went so wrong?

If I dwelled on that particular train of thought, I would possibly lose my mind. I decided that I would not question the "*Whys*?" There are times when, for sanity's sake, it just isn't advantageous to question the reason for the twists and turns in life. It's better not to think about the bad choices and poor judgment calls, all the mistakes that have affected not only my life, but also the lives of those I love. It isn't good to think about the past in prison. One's sanity depends on staying in the present, both mentally and physically.

INTAKE: CONTINUING THE MADNESS

"So, Sherral, you mean to tell me you gone-a wear this long, hot, long sleeve, thick, heavy, double knit outfit all the time, wit' your head all covered up?" Carlas felt my garment as she said 'double knit' to verify that she had that part correct. Carlas had eased her way to my bed and sat there beside me after I had finished my prayer ritual.

"Carlas, As-salaam-alaikum, and it is too early for you to be asking me questions, but yes this is my wearing apparel". I answered because I had already ascertained that Carlas could be persistent to the point of being a nuisance. I figured that by answering, she would go away. Wrong! Her next question followed. "And they say you don't go to the kitchen to eat, true dat?"

"Carlas, please, this is my quiet time, my only time to feel like I am alone", I really was not in the best of moods even after my morning prayer. "Okay, let's make a deal, I answer this one last question and you go interview someone else, deal?"

"I just wanna know is all, but okay I ain't gone bother you no more, since you so touchy."

"No, I do not eat in the kitchen. I do not eat pork or any pork by-products. I do not eat from containers that have had pork in them either. I do not use soap that has pork in it and toothpaste either."

"Soap and toothpaste have pork in them?" Carlas was astonished. "Girl you lying! I ain't never heard of dat."

"We made a deal," I interrupted, before she could go any further with her questions, "now see you later, Peace." Carlas reluctantly rose from my bed, looked around for another person whose business she could get into. She looked at me and said, "Girl, you got a life sentence and you think you ain't gone-a eat in that kitchen, you gone-a be breaking that door down inside of a week, you gotta eat, you must be crazy for real," she took a few steps and continued", and you comin' outta that mess you wearing, too." She walked away shaking her head with a smirk on her face.

"Ladies, line up by twos, it's time to be officially logged into the system" came the command from the officer responsible for continuing the intake process. She was a very tall, exceptionally pretty woman. She seemed to be about six feet tall, slender and what Louisianans called, "Creole". In other words, she could pass for a Caucasian. Her uniform hugged her body and accentuated her "coke-bottle figure. She wore her shirt inside her slacks, which was the uniform rule for all officers, but with this officer's physique, there was no other way to wear that shirt. Her hair was pulled back in a ponytail wore at the base of her neck. She appeared to make a deliberate effort to downplay her beauty, which was impossible unless she wore a sheet that covered her from head to toe. I wondered why, with her physical credits, she would take a job in a penal system. I knew she could have made much more money for much less work if she chose an occupation more suited to her good looks. I was too far away to read her nametag, but I fully intended to get her name and if I ever had the opportunity, I was going to ask her why she chose to work in a prison.

"O Lord, what now", was the question someone asked that brought my thoughts back to the matters at hand. Lucinda was the asker.

"What now?" Brenda echoed her inquiry.

"I thought I was officially logged in when I bent over and coughed," I said, referring to the strip search.

Velma added her input saying, "We shoulda been officially logged in when the judge gave us our time."

Carlas, the *"veteran convict"* schooled us, "Nope; we need to get our DOC numbers." The previous evening as we lay in our individual bunk talking, I learned that this was Carlas's fourth time in prison. "But see me, I ain't getting no new number." She gave the impression that she was delighted about having the same number for the fourth time!

Carlas informed us, "I use the same number every time I come back. Only way I'll get a new number is if I use another name, and why would I do that when everybody know me by Carlas Neill." She then recanted a story from her past, "One time, I was picked up for shop-lifting in Woolworth. *"She said she never went to jail for shoplifting"*, I thought to myself. So when I went to jail, I told the booking officer, who was new, that my name was Catrina Mayberry. Then, the lieutenant that was training him told him that was not my name and he even gave him my real name and spelled it for him. Ain't that something! So after that, I didn't try using no alias names no more."

Carlas was a motor-mouth this morning, or she wanted to make an impression on us. She already had made one with me, for I thought, "Why would anyone come back to this place . . . Four times!! Yes, indeed, she had made her impression with me. While I was lost in thought, Carlas continued, "I am a legend!" I thought again, *why would anyone want to be considered a legend in a penal environment?*

Lucinda still didn't fully understand, she asked Carlas, "Why do we have to get a number? They could use one uh the numbers I already got, social security number, bank account number, my employee number, driver's license number. Take uh pick."

Carlas was having her finest hour. She remarked, pointedly to Lucinda, "Dummy, you ain't Lucinda Gutierrez no mo'. From here on out, you gonna be known as a six-digit number. You lost that right when you done whatever you done to be in prison; whatever that was." Carlas was fishing for information. She should have known better.

"Don't get in my business, talking about what I did?" Lucinda was offended, "and my name isn't 'Dummy'.

To defuse the situation, I said, "I'll always be Sherral" I am called by a seven-letter name, not a six-digit number. Sherral is a human being, a person, a unique and wonderfully made creation made by the hands of Allah" I felt defiant about losing my identity. In truth, I surmised that I had already lost enough. I was drawing the line with my identity.

"What difference does it make what they call you, if you know who you are. Any name you got, if it isn't of African origin, isn't yours anyway." Josie had spoken. No one said anything for a long minute. We were in a brief state of acute shock.

Finally, Carlas broke the silence, "Well, you may as well get ready for another number and to be identified by that number, 'cause that's the way it is in here. You ain't out there you are in here, and we sho' ain't in Africa," Carlas glanced at Josie and continued, "and in here, you known by a number and that's that!"

"I said, 'Line up by twos'" said this beautiful officer, "You're going to the Library. Carlas, you lead the way, you know where it is," she said sarcastically.

"Yeah, you got that right, Lt. Watkins," Carlas said, "I sho do know the way.

"You should, it's like your second home," remarked Lt. Watkins, "correction, your first home, because you spend more time here than in society. I don't know why you let them release you, just stay here, you come back more than I do, and I work here!"

"Sgt. Watkins," Carlas said, pitifully, "you never did like me,"

"Line-up by twos, head out and follow Carlas." She thought for a second, then, "On second thought, don't follow Carlas, she'll lead you right back to prison." Lt. Watkins had to laugh at her own dry humor, no one else did. Few residents joined in with officers who made fun of other residents. That was one sign of unity among convicts that I noticed and appreciated.

"The Library is straight ahead so follow your nose," the lieutenant said. We started our procession to the Library.

The officer addressed Carlas, "Carlas, one thing changed in the year that you were gone, I am "Lieutenant Watkins, and it wasn't that I don't like you. I perceive that you take your freedom for granted and I see females right here that have life sentences and probably would never commit another crime again, they wish for the opportunities you have been afforded several times. You are given a privilege that I know others covet, yet you consistently return to this place". Lt. Watkins waited a few minutes before resuming. "I just don't understand it, I don't understand," she concluded shaking her head slowly. This was the end of the line for Lt. Watkins. Another officer met us as we reached the Library entrance.

"Sgt. Fletcher, how are you doing?" asked Lt. Watkins, politely.

"I'm okay, Ma'am," answered Sgt. Fletcher.

"This is six new commits to be logged into the system." said the lieutenant. "Yes Ma'am," responded Sgt. Fletcher. At that point, Lt.

Watkins left. I felt abandoned. The aura around this officer was so different from that of Lt. Watkins. Sgt. Fletcher was not a pleasant person. In fact, the aura around her was profusely pungent. That observation caused the hairs on the nape of my neck to stand up. I wondered why I had such an eerie feeling about her. The answer to my mental inquiry was soon revealed.

Sgt. Fletcher was not a nice officer at all. We realized that as soon as Lt. Watkins had left our immediate sight.

"Git behind the curtain and git in line in alphabetical order by yo' last name," she barked gruffly. Thanks to our conversations and personal introductions the night before, we had learned each other's surnames. When our shuffling into position stopped, Sgt. Fletcher said, "I need each of you to take a brown paper towel, wipe off any water, lotion, or sweat you may have on your hands." We grabbed paper towels and did as we were instructed. No one uttered a word. It was as if we were communicating with each other telepathically. I believe that my assessment of Sgt. Fletcher was shared by all. When I finished wiping my hands, I tossed the used towel into the waste basket.

"First one, come on behind the curtain and give me your full name, no aliases and no nicknames, right Carlas." Everyone surely knew Carlas. The officer smiled at Carlas, but somehow, the smile never reached her eyes. It wasn't a friendly smile. In fact, the smile Sgt. Fletcher showed gave me a sudden chill. My body shivered. For the second time I asked myself why this particular officer had such an adverse affect on me. If the saying was true, and the eyes are the mirror of the soul, Sgt. Fletcher's soul was pure evil. From her looks and the eerie feeling I got from her, I thought, *she is on the wrong side of the fence. She could easily be a convict instead of an officer.*

The curtain was a black partition that separated the Library area from the finger printing area where we were. In this area, there was a single chair and a school-type desk that held sectioned fingerprint paper, an inkpad, a stack of paper towels and a box of facial tissues. On the floor in a corner, was a black waste paper basket that had a collection of brown paper towels, and facial tissue. Some of the towels had smeared black ink on them. It was apparent that the officer made little or no effort toward tidying the area up. It was my assumption that she had even contributed to the area's state of disorder.

When it came my turn to disappear behind the curtain, I had the nagging suspicion that no matter what I said or did, no matter how silent and polite I tried to be, there was going to be a confrontation with this mean character. I said to myself, *"Sherral, just be quiet. Don't say anything. You already have the reputation of being a "smart-mouth".*

"Name," the sergeant looked at me as if I had come from the pits of hell. I looked back at her.

"Your name I said!" she barked at me. I prepared to deposit my most polite and submissive voice into this situation. I cleared my throat and said, "Sherral Kahey is my name, Ma'am. What is your name?" Straightway, I knew the latter should not have been spoken.

"You don't ask my name, Kahey, you just answer what I ask you, got dat!" She spat those words at me as if they tasted like bitter herbs. She continued, "Your reputation precedes you. You one of dim biggety baby killers. You got a lot of nerve coming here trying to act like you Miss Somebody, you ain't nothin' or nobody." She was right in my face. She was furious. This woman had a serious rage embedded within her heart. She appeared to be mad at the world.

"Ma'am, all I did was asked your name trying to be polite and make conversation," I said, trying to neutralize the situation. She continued her tongue-lashing enjoying every word of it.

"You the lowest of the low, the worst of the worse, get outta here and git to the dead end of the line. Maybe by then, I will have cooled off enough not to break your fingers," she said.

"But, but I . . . I . . ." I really wanted to apologize although I didn't know what I had done that required an apology.

"No buts, do it now! Right freakin' now! with your smart mouth. You baby killing, life doing scumbag. They shoulda gave you the death penalty. Git outta my face, NOW!" I had learned the officer's name, but I had a few names in my head that I would have liked to call her. This officer, in just these few minutes, had pronounced a label on me that I would have a difficult time amending, if I chose to do so.

"Ma'am, you got me wrong, I said trying to correct whatever I had done wrongly, "I . . . I

She cut me off, again, "You have a direct order to shut up and get out of my face, Convict!"

I lowered my head for an instant, them something within me said, *"Hold you head up!"*

I obeyed that voice that would ultimately guide me throughout my incarceration.

Strolling from behind that curtain with the swagger of a proud peahen, I moved to the end of the line as I was instructed. I did not avoid eye contact with anyone; I smiled as if I were promenading down a fashion show runway.

After obeying that inner voice, I made a decision that had an integral role in my smooth transformation from freedom to life. I based my mental and emotional adjustment on the precept that no matter what, I would not allow what people said to or about me cause me to react in a negative manner. I would respond if, and only if, I deemed it necessary. I knew who and what I was and I refused to allow anyone to strip me of my pride and dignity the way I had been stripped physically earlier. I came to prison with the qualities of a strong black woman and I determined early in my imprisonment that I would be released with those and even greater virtues.

"Girl, what did you say to that woman?" whispered an inmate I did not know. She was a tall, dark-skinned female who looked as if she could have been one of the maintenance workers . . . to clarify, MALE maintenance workers! She braided her hair to the back of her head in thick cornrows. She was wearing denim overalls and a blindingly white tee shirt.

"OH hi, I'm Billy" she introduced herself. She went further saying, "I heard that raucous back there with you and her, but I could only hear her loud mouth".

"I would rather not discuss it right now, Billy", I wanted Billy to go away. I did not want this mean officer to see me talking to another inmate. It would only give her more reason to be nasty. Then I thought, *"What the hell, she didn't have a reason to be nasty toward me in the first place."* I explained, "Well, all I did was asked her for her name." I didn't feel like talking at the moment, but in light of my new revelation, I talked because it was not the obedient thing to do. I was rebelling in my small way and feeling good for doing it. We could not have any contact with other inmates until we had been "cleared". That was the standard procedure for all females entering the facility, but ha-ha, I was talking to another inmate before I had been cleared, so what!

Cleared was another prison term that means we had to receive a physical, medical and mental evaluation before we would be able to interact with the general population. We had to have a clean bill of health. Although I did not feel particularly sociable, I had already alienated myself from the officers, I surely did not need dissention from the other inmates.

"Look," Billy said, "I work here in the Library, so if you need anything, let me know."

"Thanks," I replied, "but I won't need anything," I wasn't falling into that old prison trap.

Everything in the system comes with a price.

Oddly, for the remainder of the day, no one said a word, especially to me. When we returned to the Infirmary, where we were housed, I went to my bed and lied down flat on my back and I stared at the dingy, rain-stained tiled ceiling. This had been a long, tiresome day for me. For the first time, I felt like an outsider with women who had embraced me affectionately prior to the encounter behind the "curtain".

There were prejudices inside the penal system that had nothing to do with the color of one's skin. The guard had said that I was the *"lowest of the low."* To translate her words in light of my current quandary, all felons were considered low, but those convicted of child-related charges were considered the lowest, the oddballs, and outcasts. Facing a life sentence, I felt I had bigger fish to fry than to be concerned with how people viewed me.

If it meant that I had to walk the compound alone, so be it. I was not born a twin. I came to this facility alone and I felt that I could do my time alone. Who was I kidding; I was offended that these women whom I had bonded with previously, now had nothing to say to me. They didn't even try to console me following my time of humiliation, nor did they join the ranks, and resort to name-calling, anything would have been better at this point than the silence that had culminated throughout this infirmary.

In this single day, I had been humiliated by an officer; a lesbian had befriended me; and I was ostracized by the only friends I thought I had in this cold, cold dark world. What a day! What a life! What a hand I had been dealt. Well, who said that life was anything even remotely related to fair? Survivors in the penal structure made the best of the hands they were dealt. The weak ones whined about their hands and tried to show everyone how unfair their hands were. The strong ones faced each day with their hands and the ups and downs that came with the day. The strong ones made the best they could from a bad situation without comment.

GENERAL POPULATION

Subsequent to the intake process, all new commits are released to general population, assigned a room, and, at least, one other roommate, and the most significant part, given a job. In prison everyone works. It doesn't matter about one's mental, physical, or emotional state of being. Work is mandatory. If you do not work, you go to lockdown. You are placed in a cell, your mattress and any bedding in the cell is taken from you for the duration of the workday.

After intake, unless all the new commits are placed in the same dormitory, and or on the same job, we don't see much of each other. In light of the way we split, I was content not seeing them. I needed time to get over the pain I'd felt our last evening together. Therefore, when I learned that we were going to the same dorm, I wasn't the happiest camper.

This day was filled with what the "establishment" had scheduled us to do. I was placed in the new commit dormitory with the others, to my dismay. The saving fact was that we were not in the same immediate area. So, I could avoid seeing them, not that I did not want to see them or that I did not like them. It was just the fact that they averted eye contact with me, and when they did that, it evoked anger in me.

I was moved to Gemini-2 annex. This was once a game and television area that had been turned into a "make-shift" dormitory. It was full of beds and footlockers. There were about 25 females housed in this opened area.

Upon my arrival on Gemini-2, a loud voice rang out piercing my ears, "Hey! Sister, over here, I got you a bed." At the end of that voice was a huge, broad and bold black female who looked like the black version of Big Bird. I ignored her and went to the control station to report to the officer, which was what I was instructed to do when I was released from the infirmary.

"Sarge", I said. I started to say, *Ma'am*, but using that form of acknowledgment had gotten me in a world of trouble on more than one occasion. I repeated, "Sarge, I was told to report to you." I used my most self-effacing voice. The officer slowly raised her head from the novel she was reading and said," What am I suppose to do with you?" I opted not to answer that question because my response would surely have been legitimately sarcastic. She looked at me, up and down, then said, "Didn't you hear LilliePearl say that she had your bed? What you worrying me for?" So, the loud-mouthed "welcome wagon's" name was LilliePearl.

"Sarge," I said.

She cut me off, "Don't call me "Sarge, don't bother me! Don't disturb me? Don't even look at me. Just get to your bunk and leave me alone." She cut me off before I could say another word. I walked away thinking there was a conspiracy to drive me crazy. I didn't know what to say, I didn't know how to address the officers, I didn't know where to go or what to do. The feeling of despair was settling in my psyche as easily as I was settling into this environment.

"Sister, I told you I had your bed," LilliePearl said. I just looked at her. She kept talking. "My name is LilliePearl. It's all one name like "LilliePearl" one long name. Why you looking at me like that? I ain't gonna bite you. I'ma big girl, but I don't eat no people. I jest wanna be yo'friend." LilliePearl seemed to be a cordial person, but

I had heard enough about prison-life to know to be aware of overly friendly females. They always wanted something.

"No offense, but do I look like I need a friend?" I didn't give her the opportunity to reply; "I'm not looking for any friends all I want to do is my time and get on outta here".

"Well, you sho' got a lotta time to do," LilliePearl retorted irreverently.

"Whatever time I have is my business, and like I said, I do not need friends." LilliePearl had rubbed me the wrong way, talking about my time. That was not appropriate prison etiquette, if there were such a thing. I made up my mind that I was not going to like this person.

"I got three years and I'm almost through doing my time. You just started yours. Believe me, 'fore it's over, you'll need friends." LilliePearl didn't seem angry about my rebuff. I went to the bunk that LilliePearl had previously indicated. I began taking what was left of my belongings from the black garbage bag that I had been.

LilliePearl sat on her bunk, which was right across from mine. She watched as I unpacked. I was given one footlocker to store my property. After the officers had trashed most of my items, I had very little. Yet, even with what I had left, it was still a feat to arrange my belongings neatly in the small space provided for me.

"LilliePearl, if I did choose a friend, it would not be someone who was getting ready to get out." I said matter-of-factly. LilliePearl did not respond to my statement. I thought she hadn't heard. She continued to stare at me. "Why are you watching me, "I asked her.

"These my eyes, and I look wherever I want. And sometimes it's good to have a friend who is getting out so they can run for ya," LilliePearl had heard, then she said, "Why are you so angry?" That question struck me like a thunderbolt. *Why was I angry?* I could think of several reasons off the top of my head, but none of the reasons for my anger had anything to do with LilliePearl.

"Look, LilliePearl, I apologize for being crass with you," I said. "It's just that I have had a hard time these few days and I am on edge, but it has nothing to do with you,"

"Grass? What you mean by 'grass with me'? Lillie Pearl's face was contorted. She was perplexed and for a brief moment, so was I.

Then, "I said crass not grass." I had to smile this time. I explained, "Crass means insensitive or not caring about your feelings."

"Okay, then, you sho' was crass with me for no reason." LilliePearl was proud to use the word. She continued, "Ain't nothing wrong with having friends. Sister, by the way, what is your name?"

I'm Sherral Kahey", I answered without protest or embellishments. I'm sure that, by now, everybody at LCIW knew my name from the incident in the Library. I also knew that I would not have any problems staying away from people.

OH! Yeah, I heard of you." As LilliePearl recognized the name, I braced myself for the verbal insults that I thought would surely follow. She continued to say, "Yeah, you that Muslim sister that don't eat no pork. Damn, I shoulda knew that by the way you dressed."

My transitional Islamic dress was a two-piece culottes-type pant skirt that came to my ankles, a long-sleeved tunic top that covered my neck, and a headdress much like the ones nuns wore. My garments were made in the same style but in a variety of colors.

"Where they put you to work?" LilliePearl inquired.

"They put me on the line crew." I replied, accepting that LilliePearl was not going to leave me alone.

"Sister, I know they ain't put you on no line crew. Say it ain't so!" LilliePearl seemed genuinely concerned.

"That's where they put me and that's where I will be working."
I countered.

"Well, I guess you better git some more clothes, cause you gonna
burn up in all that knit you got on," LilliePearl laughed.

"You better keep your day job, cause you'll never make it as a
comedian." I responded, not seeing the humor in what LilliePearl
had said.

"It ain't no joke, and all I was doing was giving you some advice."
LilliePearl said, her face still holding a remnant of the laugh she had
just enjoyed.

"I didn't ask for nor do I need advice, I can take care of myself."
My face felt hot. LilliePearl was relentless. She kept talking, "This
is August, the hottest month in the year and they done put you on the
line crew, Sister, they trying to kill you. I heard you had already made
some enemies with the cops. You better call your family, TODAY"

"LilliePearl, you ever seen the people who live in the deserts, or
anywhere in the Middle East?" I was trying to sound patient, but I
was quickly coming unraveled.

"Yeah, I sho' have, but you ain't no Arab, and this sho' ain't the
desert or the Middle East." Now, the laughter had vanished, replaced
with concern with the same intensity of the laughter.

My head was beginning to throb. All I wanted to do was get on
with my day. I wanted LilliePearl, her laughter and her concern to
disappear, but she was not going to accommodate me. LilliePearl
was bossy and pushy. She reminded me of someone, but I couldn't
think right now, who it was.

"LilliePearl, I'll worry about that when the time comes, okay.
Thank you for your concern, but I'll be fine, now please may I have
some privacy?" I had hoped that being superficially polite would
have moved her to comply.

LilliePearl emitted a hardy guffaw, "Privacy, where you gonna get that in here? Have you looked around you? This ain't the Sheraton, Sister, you is in an opened dormitory." LilliePearl laughed rather than spoke that statement. Everyone in the area was looking at us.

"LilliePearl, you have a direct order to lower your voice!" yelled the officer who had been reading the novel in the control station. She had left the control office and was standing in the immediate area near our bunks.

"Okay Miss Wright, but you woulda laughed out loud too, if you hadda heard the joke Sister just cracked" LilliePearl answered, still laughing. "She is one funny lady!"

When Miss Wright left the area to return to her novel, LilliePearl looked at me and said, "Sister, you got a lot to learn; now I will leave you alone, but you will not have any privacy. She walked away laughing uncontrollably. LilliePearl returned to her bunk and lied down to read a book that had been lying on her bed. I continued to settle in to prison life. Each time I looked up from my task, someone was watching me. One other lesson that I would have to learn was to ignore the constant eyes that would be upon me. My attire surely didn't help; my charge was another reason for stares, not to mention the encounter that I had had with the officer in the Library. One thing was a certainty; people were going to stare at me. It was my task to get used to it. Officers were always looking at us, but I never imagined that other offenders like myself, would be giving me the stares. One way or other, eyes would be on me for the rest of my life. I wondered if I would ever become so desensitized that the stares would not disturb me. I hoped not.

"As-Salaam-Alaikum, Sister", that was a familiar Islamic greeting that I thought I'd never hear again. As-Salaam-Alaikum is the Islamic greeting that means "Peace be with you." I turned to see a female dressed in a long skirt, white blouse and a scarf on her head.

"Wa-Alaikum-Salaam," I replied. "Wa-Alaikum-Salaam," is the appropriate response which means, "peace be with you also.

"I'm Sister LaGerda and I know who you are, everybody know you." LaGerda chimed.

"Well, I'm glad to meet you, Sister LaGerda." I replied again.

"Did you know that they have a Muslim service here every Saturday at 9 o'clock?" LaGerda asked me.

"No, I didn't know that," I was surprised to hear that bit of news.

LaGerda continued, "Yeah, they have two brothers and a sister that come here for the service. They'll be here this Saturday. Wanna come with me?"

"Well, I'll come to see what it's about, thanks for inviting me." I said.

"Okay As-Salaam-Alaikum, Sista." LaGerda concluded and left.

"Wa-Alaikum-Salaam, Sister LaGerda," I responded in kind.

I had seen LaGerda a few times but I never thought she was Islamic because I'd seen her dressed as she was today. I had also seen her wearing Western attire without head covering. When I thought of LaGerda, the word "confused" came to mind. At any rate, I thought attending the meeting couldn't hurt. I'd go to see what it was about. I went about my day without seeing LaGerda again. The next morning immediately following my Fard (Morning Prayer), "As-Salaam-Alaikum, Sista." It was LaGerda. I replied in kind.

"Sista, they say you put your baby in a oven," whispered LaGerda in my ear. I just looked at her. She continued, "Yeah, they say, you beat her and when she wouldn't quit crying that's when you put her in the oven so you couldn't hear her crying. Then you forgot she were in the oven and turned it on." That ain't true is it?"

I was appalled at the fact that Sister LaGerda would bring such non-sense to me this early in the morning. I opened my mouth to speak, "Sister LaGerda, they do not know me or about why I am here. All they know is what they heard and what their imaginative minds have told them,"

"Sista, I gotta go get ready for work." LaGerda said as she departed my presence.

"As-salaam-alaikum," I said as she left.

"Oh, yeah, Sista, Wa-alaikum-salaam."

I didn't see LaGerda anymore that day.

De`jivu`, the next morning as I completed my prayer ritual, here comes LaGerda.

"Sista, As-Salaam-alaikum. Girl, you ain't gonna believe what they said at breakfast." LaGerda exclaimed. I didn't want to hear it, but LaGerda wanted to say it, she continued, "They said that you choked your baby and put him in a trash can." Yesterday it was a girl, today it's a boy. I looked eye-to-eye at LaGerda. She said, "Is that true, that ain't true is it?"

"Look, Sister LaGerda, these females do not say a word to me. They do not have the nerve to come in my face and confront me about anything one way or other. They are not woman enough. So don't you ever again come to me telling me anything you heard at breakfast, lunch or dinner about me from them", I said all in one breath. If it doesn't come to my ears from their mouths, then don't you ever again be their carrier, is that understood?" I concluded and felt much better for it.

"Sister Sherral, all I was doing was keepin' you up on what "they" say", she defended herself. I could tell from LaGerda's expression that she was shocked at my frankness.

"LaGerda, I could care less what "they" say about me. My dearly departed Grandmother once told me that a dog that will bring a bone to your yard would take one from your yard. That means the person who is always bringing mess will also take back mess. I have nothing to say about them or my charge to them or to you." I meant that and I did not care that I had offended LaGerda. She did not care about how I felt about hearing what "they" were saying. From that day forward, LaGerda never told me anything that "they" were saying and no one else ever confronted me about my charge. They gossiped and whispered, but, fortunately, I was not privy to their conversations. My concern was doing my time and getting out of this place.

WORK DAYS

My first work day began at 4:45 a.m. when every inmate had to wake up, get out of bed, stand beside her bed, and remain there until the counting officer completed her count of the female offenders in the immediate area. The process of counting the dormitory area took about ten minutes if the officer counted correctly the first time. By the time she announced, "Count Clear" which meant we could go back to our beds, not many of us were able to resume our sleep state. If the count was not what the roster indicated, the process was repeated. There were times when the inmates stood for as much as half an hour until the count was correct or until it was ascertained that someone had escaped.

"Morning, Sister, what did you say your name is, I forgot", that was my new friend, LilliePearl. "I keep wanting to call you Kathy Kates and I know that ain't right," she said.

"As-Salaam Alaikum, forgotting my name, might be an indication that you may not need to pursue a friendship with me", I suggested.

"Sister, I know you didn't just cuss me, what did you say?" LilliePearl demanded, "I heard you say something about ass. I ain't done nothin' for you to be cussin' me out early in the morning." LilliePearl was genuinely offended.

This time, it was my turn to emit the loud burst of laughter, "No, LilliePearl," I said as my laughing subsided, 'As-salaam-alaikum' is the Arabic greeting instead of saying "Good Morning" it means

Peace be with you." When I say that to you, your response is, Wa-alaikum-salaam and that means peace be with you also."

"Here you go with the Arabic stuff again," LilliePearl was annoyed, "you ain't no Arab", she pronounced the word, "*A-Rab*". "You having some kinda identity crisis or something." She was trying to gaze deep into my eyes as if she could read my mind through my eyes. Lillie Pearl was nose-to-nose with me, gazing into my face.

"That is how I greet people, not every morning or afternoon or evening is a good one, but everybody needs "peace" in their life, don't you agree?" I was explaining to LilliePearl because I just could not get rid of her, so why not teach her some Islam while she was in my company.

"Yeah, I guess. I never looked at it that way." LilliePearl still looked to be baffled. After a moment, she said cheerfully, "Well so much for the lesson in A-rab language. Let's go to breaffass."

LilliePearl went back to her bunk and grabbed wrinkled clothes to put on. She pulled her gown off, revealing a body clothed in bra and panties only. She dressed as she continued to talk to me, in front of God, the officers and every female who was brave enough to look upon that body. I had chosen to turn my head.

When a majority of the females had left to go to breakfast, I went to the restroom and did my ablution. An ablution is the ritual washing of the hand, face and head cavities (as I learned recently that they were called) in preparation of entering the presence of Allah.

Upon returning to my bunk I stood facing the direction of the rising sun-East, placed my out-stretched arms in front of me, palms opened and upward, bowed my head and began to recite the Morning Prayer. Muslims around the world performed this activity every morning at five a.m. When I completed my prayer, I turned to see that every female on the floor officers and offenders alike, had me in their sights. I smiled at some of them and went about my business. Yes, I could understand what LilliePearl meant when she said there was no privacy. If a person could not have some privacy during prayer, when could she?

At about 6:45 in the morning, all those assigned to the line crew were gathering at the back gate for the roll call. There were about 50 females dressed in denim jeans and various colored shirts, blouses, halters and tank tops. Then there were the lockdown females, which accounted for an additional 25 females. They were dressed in black-and white stripes. The proverbial "prison" stripes uniforms.

At 7 o'clock, there was a male officer on a horse who called us by name, one-by-one. As our names were called we went out the back gate that was opened, we held our arms straight up in the air, opened our legs, wide, as the back gate officer pat frisked us. This officer ran her hands over our bodies from head to toe. If she felt something that was suspicious, you then had to show her what it was, or you were taken to lockdown. Additionally, if what you had was not allowed, you were taken to lockdown.

Three officers were the only ones going into the field with about 75 female offenders. The officer on the horse was the ranking officer. He was the first man I had seen on the compound. His name was **Lt. Bromwell**. He was a long, slender man who favored the horse he was riding, but the women sought after him. They thought he was sexy. I could not see sexy unless you were a female horse! He had dark brown skin, ashy black hair that looked like it needed combing and he wore one of those "Smokey the bear" hats. He wore dark sunglasses and the traditional uniform of the correctional officers with one exception, he had a thick, double stranded red cord circling his left shoulder. I learned later that the red cord rope signified his ability to take an inmate down. In other words, he was trained in defensive tactics. The inmates called it the "ass-kicking" squad. These were the officers who were called in to "handle" disruptions and disruptors.

Officer Number 2 handed us tools. She was a young Caucasian who looked as if she had just graduated from high school. To reiterate my summation, the officer was wearing a high school graduation ring. She had long, thick locks of brown, wavy hair that she wore loose held off her face with black hair combs on either side of her head behind her ears. Her eyes were green and set too close to the bridge of her large nose. She must have melted in her uniform. It was as tight as a second skin. It was so tight that I imagined she must have had trouble breathing. She had full lips for a Caucasian, and her figure wasn't half-bad, except she did have the flat rear, so typical of her race of women. Her name was **Sgt. Wiley**. Sgt. Wiley smiled a lot and I even saw her making eyes at the lieutenant. I figured she must have had a crush on him along with over half the females on the line crew. This officer wasn't bad looking and I knew she could have done better than horse-face Bromwell. Beauty is in the eyes of the beholder. As my sainted grandmother used to say, "*So is ugly.*"

The third officer directed us where to stand until all the others were ready to go to work and watched us as a hawk watches a chicken. I was convinced she was aware of the danger. This officer could have been someone's grandmother. She looked to be in her mid-fifties; her hair was cut short and was mingled gray and black. She was heavy, yet curvy and she wore her uniform well, a very neat women, she wore a very light facial foundation. Her lips were painted red as were her long fingernails. She had long eyelashes that appeared to be false. Her name was **Master Sgt. Kellard**. This officer was a heavy smoker. In the length of time we had been out, she had smokes four cigarettes, back-to-back.

Ironically, all the offenders were given tools such as yard rakes, hoes, axes, sling blades, and shovels. We were considered hardened criminals. Those on lockdown were considered especially hardened, rebellious, and even mentally disturbed. Yet we were given extremely lethal "tools" that could have been turned into weapons at any given time. That was a scary thought for me because I thought about what could happen in an opened field with only three security officers, none of which had weapons, one of them was on a horse, and 75 'criminals' with tools that were potential weapons.

"Hey you! You! You smoke?" someone said. I looked around to see who was talking and to whom she was referring. I was the intended recipient of that inquiry.

"No, I don't smoke", I answered the lady in black-and-white stripes. As sarcastic as I had been portrayed, I was not about to get my "flip" on with this roughneck.

"Damn, it bad when they start gibbin' nuns time!" Roughneck said then laughed. I did not answer her. It didn't matter, she kept going, "So, what you did?" she quizzed, "drop the priest's holy water; or was you trying to drop your draws for da priest, Yeah, I heared 'bout you hot nuns" She laughed at her own off-color jokes. When her guffaws subsided, she got back to her original thought, "You ain't got no smokes, you say," she repeated herself.

I repeated myself, "No, I don't smoke". Without another word, Roughneck walked off, sling blade in hand.

It was a hot day and the officers had brought a huge water cooler out with them for us to have cold water to drink. Two inmates got the 'privilege' of carrying the cooler. The 'privilege' in carrying the cooler was two-fold. First, you were permitted to sit in the shade and issue the cups of water. Then, you could sit around the lieutenant who stayed on his horse. The girls fought over who the lucky one would be. We were instructed not to throw our cups away because we only got one cup a day. These were thin paper cups that barely held up on a good day. They had to use their nametags to clip the cups to their shirts. If a female lost her cup for whatever reason, she wasn't given another one unless the one issuing the cups was her friend. Usually the water bearer did not have any friends that day. Therefore, the person who lost the cup was out of luck, she had to go without water or drink from her usually dirty cupped hands. I did not drink water at all.

"O Sister," I looked around to see none other than LilliePearl.

"Sherral", I gave my name as if she had asked me for it.

"Yeah, well, it should be Sour Sherral," LilliePearl responded. "Look, it's too hot for that mess, do you want some water" She had two cups in her hand.

"No, but thank you for asking," I replied, "I'm not thirsty."

"Girl, I know you lying! We been out here for four hours, almost and you ain't drink no water, I been lookin' at cha'". LilliePearl cared.

"I am not thirsty." I restated.

"You gonna die out here for sho'", she concluded., "first you got on that blanket of clothes, then you not sweatin then you ain't taken no water. You gone die of hydration."

"De-hydration", I corrected her.

"That's what I said," she lied.

"Please stop worrying about me, LilliePearl," I was moved by her concern, but I was irritated none-the-less, "I've been wearing this outfit for eleven years in all kind of weather and under all sort of conditions and circumstances." Today, I really wanted LilliePearl to leave me alone. I had to concentrate on all these inmates with all these 'weapons'.

"You ever been in prison?" she asked, persistently. I refused to answer her. I thought maybe if I ignored her, she would go away.

She didn't go away, instead she said, "You don't know how you'll react in this situation cause you have never been in this situation before,"

"LilliePearl, I don't want any water, I don't want to talk, and I don't want any friends. I just want to be left alone, do you understand that!" I had had enough of LilliePearl.

Just as LilliePearl was about to answer, "Bitch, you do got a cigarette, I just seen the smoke coming off-en it! You lyin' Ho', you!" That was Roughneck. She was speaking to a female who looked every bit as rough as she did. Both women were wielding "tools". *"Lord, Allah, someone is about to die, today!"* I thought.

"HO', I said I ain't got no smokes. Now get outta my face 'fore I cut another pussy in your head!" These fiery words came from a female who looked every bit as menacing as "Roughneck". Straightway, I moved away to the far end of the field. I noticed as I moved away from the 'action' that Lt. Brown positioned his horse in my direction. The two officers on foot approached the perpetrators. I thought to myself, *"These officers are either very brave or very stupid."* Both roughnecks had "tools" in their hands. Neither officer had anything to protect or defend herself. Sgt. Wiley stepped right between the women while Msgt. Kellard stepped behind Roughneck No. 1, the one who asked me for a cigarette. All the while, Lt. Bromwell kept his eyes on the situation and his horse facing my direction.

At my safe vantage point, I could not hear what the officers said to the women, but whatever was said must have been funny because they all cackled so loudly that the horse began to arouse and the lieutenant calmed him, continuing to keep the horse turned toward my general location. Sometime later, I noticed the same two females laughing and talking as if nothing had taken place between them. They seemed to be the best of friends . . . now. I had feared for someone's life to the point that I was afraid for all of us. One of the other inmates let me in on a secret that really caught me by surprise.

She whispered, "Hey Sista, come close."

I wasn't sure I wanted to be close to her, I asked, "What's wrong?"

"You may be in trouble, that's what's wrong? Come here" she insisted. It sounded so urgent that I resisted the urge not to comply with her request. I came closer.

She was still whispering, "Uh-member when Drucilla and Zemia was fussing and you walked down to the other end of the field?"

"Yes I was trying to get away from the action. Which one was which" I said.

"I'll jest put it this way, the gorilla was Drucilla, the big ugly one" she remarked, and chuckled.

"Well, anyway' Lt. Bromwell reported to the Assistant Warden of Security that he thought you mighta been trying to escape," she was still whispering but I heard her loud and clear.

"Escape! ME! No, you have me mixed up with someone else," I could not believe my ears.

"You the only 'Mooz-lem' on the line crew, "she had stopped whispering and was looking around to see if she had an audience other than me. Her hands were on her hips.

"How do you know that?" I inquired.

"'Cause I work the water today and when Lt. Bromwell rode his horse back to the shade tree where I was, he got on the radio and called to report that you looked suspicious, like you might be thinking about running." This person spoke matter-of-factly.

"How do you know he was talking about me?" I could not believe what I was hearing.

"He didn't know your name, so he called you the "black nun-lookin convict", she was glad to be relaying what could be some valuable information.

"What happens now," I asked, "I mean, will something happen to me?" now it was my turn to whisper. I don't know why I felt that I needed to whisper, but I felt secretive.

"Nothin' but they gonna be watching you, like crazy." Then she just walked away.

She left me with my thoughts. Two "tool" wielding convicts were in a heated confrontation and all the lieutenant could focus on was me? I just wanted to be far away from the danger, and he had viewed me as the potential danger. What a day!

The following day, the line crew workers were led into a densely wooded area about three miles behind the back gate area. Added to our list of "tools" were about five saws.

We were no sooner in the woods when all hell broke loose. "Ho, yo Maw is the bitch, Bitch, now what you gonna do? I done got in the dozens wit' yo ass." Drucilla, aka Roughneck, was the culprit once again. I could see why she was on lockdown, what I did not understand is why they allowed her to come out with the line crew. Drucilla had chosen a different victim this time.

"You sad, sorry-ass, gorilla-alike, broke, broke-down, bumming, begging, lost and forgotten, thrower-away, unloved, unwanted, reject!" the victim said in one long breath. I think she stopped to breathe then she continued, "You put your hands, or that ax in your hands on me, and your mammy won't be able to recognize that ugly mug of yours."

This "victim" was a short petite female who must have had the instincts of a giant or she thought she was bigger than she actually was. Drucilla walked slowly to this person, saying, "Octavia, I asked you a simple question and you had to git smart wit' me. All I was asking you is do you have a cigarette and you come getting smart."

"I got cigarettes, keep 'em and you still ain't gitting one, not even the short." Octavia was not relenting nor was she afraid. *Was it because she had a shovel in her hands?*

The 'short' of a cigarette was the last pull or puffs of a cigarette closest to the filter or your finger, depending on what you were smoking. The least expensive cigarettes were what a females called "roll-'em-ups. Those were the pouches of cigarette tobacco with about 40 thin rolling papers. Octavia wasn't smoking a "roll-'em-up.

Octavia took a cigarette from her jeans pocket, lit it with a match that was also in her pocket, took about four long drags, and then did something that I thought was the craziest move ever. Octavia took the cigarette from her mouth, blew thick smoke in Drusilla's face, threw the half-smoke cigarette to the ground, gave Drucilla a wicked smile, and crushed the cigarette into the ground.

I retreated to my distant viewing point this time moving closer to the location where Lt. Bromwell sat on his horse. Drucilla stood there in utter shock. Her mouth was wide opened as she glared at Octavia's boot crushing the cigarette into the ground to make sure Drucilla would not get a grain of tobacco. Drucilla advanced toward Octavia still holding the ax in her clutched fist. I was positive that some blood was going to be shed.

"Bitch, you don't talk 'bout my mama, you dick-lickin dog!" Drucilla was furious and her anger had nothing to do with her mother. "I'll stomp a mud-hole in your ass for talking about my mama who birthed me." Roughneck was livid.

Octavia did not back up or attempt to defuse the situation. "Magilla Gorilla Drucilla, your mammy shoulda flushed you and raised the after-birth!" Everyone laughed; Roughneck was losing this verbal battle. Octavia and Drucilla were walking toward each other neurotically. My heart was pounding to the beat of each of their steps. The officers were observing this altercation, nonchalantly. Lt. Bromwell never took his eyes off me!

Msgt. Kellard began trotting toward the pair followed closely by Sgt. Wiley. Lt. Bromwell seemed oblivious to the problem at hand. He was focused on my whereabouts.

By the time the officers reached the two arguing females, they were about five feet apart. Both officers stepped between them.

Kellard spoke loudly and clearly, "You two want to be locked up?" she asked. Drucilla was already locked up, that was not a threat for her.

"Naw, I ain't getting locked up behind this nothing-ass bitch!" barked Octavia, "I'm gonna stay out here on the compound where I can smoke."

"Bitch ain't got the heart to do no lockdown time," retorted Drucilla.

"That's enough of that! You both have a direct order to get busy working or I'll get the jewelry!" said Msgt. Kellard. Both women got calm and quiet "tools" still in hand.

Jewelry, in prison, is not 14 Karat gold or beautiful sterling silver. Jewelry was the restraints used to transport inmates either inside or outside the confines of the facility. No offender in her right mind wanted restraints. Being locked up was bad enough, being put in restraints and placed in an 8x6 cold, steel-walled cell with a concrete slab for a bed was indeed an insult added to injury. When the "jewelry" was introduced into an altercation that meant that someone was being taken to the lockdown area and placed on what was called "Administrative Segregation" or A.S.

"Hey, Drucilla," Octavia called out to her "all they know to do is lock a nigga up, huh, Girl"

"Uh-huh, a person can't even have a friendly disagreement wit-out the cops wanting to threaten us," said Drucilla, sheepishly.

I could not believe what I was seeing and hearing, these women were just moments from inflicting great bodily harm or worse killing each other. Now they were calling each other sister.

"Drew, you wanna share a smoke with me?" whispered Octavia.

Yeah, Sista, I sho' would like a smoke, Kellard done worked my nerves up!" replied Drucilla.

Octavia pulled out a pack of Kool 100s and gave one of them to Drucilla. They walked away smiling, talking and puffing on their cigarettes as if nothing had taken place between them.

I learned a valuable lesson from observing that encounter. I understood why watching me, as Lt. Bromwell had done was of more urgency that the confrontation at hand. The women were afraid of words from the officers such as, "direct order" 'lockdown"; "the jewelry"; "report"; "write-up". These women walked the "red-light" district in some of the most dangerous cities in America. They walked the street in the wee hours of the morning searching for drugs, sex, or both. Women who wielded glocks, uzzies, knives even axes; women who fought men, policemen officers, women who boldly walked in stores and stole with no thought of what could happen to them; women who robbed banks at gunpoint, were literally terrified of these words. I wondered why. This fear that I saw in so many offenders did not make sense to me but it was unquestionably the reality.

Showing fear or any type of negative emotion in prison was not a good or wise thing to do. Fear was considered weak. Crying was also viewed as weak. Weakness was a disease that would eventually destroy you mentally and emotionally. The strong did not prey on the weak, the weak preyed on those that were weaker than they were. The strong stayed to themselves, obeyed the rules, did their time and got out. They maintained a level of distance from the others while keeping a rapport with both officers and offenders. The strong cried and showed other emotions, but there was a way to do that. The strong knew that "night-time was the "right-time" to let it go. If the strong did not have an outlet, they would have lost their minds. The strong devised methods of showing emotion yet keeping their dignity. They were no nonsense people. This world was a place of diverse people thrust together and expected to co-exist in a world designed to destroy all of us.

Such was the life I was assigned to live. Life, bars, and barbed-wire, a world within a world. A world that few would ever come to understand, few would even care to understand and yet, a world that would surely touch the lives of the masses in one form or other.

Thereafter, the next few months were a collection of learning, adjusting, re-adjusting and adapting. I learned to ignore the looks and stares of the officers and the inmates. I adjusted to living in an opened area where someone was watching you all the time. I adapted to the conditions and the environment. I learned to ignore the arguments that were loud and full of profanity. I knew that they were just blowing off steam. The verbal explosion was the length of the altercations. I also learned that prison was full of good people who just went the wrong way for various reason. Some were here as the result of following and standing by their "man". Some were here as a result of being beaten and battered by their "man". Yes, there were a few mental and emotional issues, but for the most part,

I had met some sad stories in the form of female offenders. I learned to look beyond their tough outer shell into the hearts of women who never dreamed of spending time in prison. These females, like myself, had aspirations, plans, goals and desires. Not one of us made the conscious decision to become felony offenders.

CONTINUED CUSTODY

"Sherral Kahey, report to the Classification officer immediately, "was the call from a feminine voice over the public announcement system. When "immediately" was added to an announcement that meant the person who wanted to see you did not want to wait until you arrived. It meant, "hurry-up to wait". Staff deemed it degrading to have to wait on the offenders, so they have us waiting for hours while they did whatever staff personnel did to fill the hours in a day. Immediate meant we hurry and they take their time. After all, we had the "time" to wait. The P.A. announcer would say "immediately" so that you would make haste to get there. The problem with that system of management was that it did not take long for the offenders to figure out the real meaning of "immediately."

Immediately meant that the offender would have to wait for the administrative person. So, the impact of the word was of non-effect after about the first two or three times. I had learned that lesson the first time I was out of breath trying to reach a location, "immediately". I sat there for thirty minutes waiting for the person who had called for me.

"Hey, Sista, they paging you." Of course that was my friend, LilliePearl. "What they want wit'cha'?"

"Look, how do I know what they want?" I said irritated first that she always seemed to be there and secondly because she always seemed to be in my business.

"Well, you ain't asked for no job change, did cha'?" she inquired.

"LilliePearl, now why would I ask for a job change and get out of the hot sun, the mosquitoes, and the crazy women with dangerous tools that substitute for weapons?" I was being derisive. "This is too much fun! I'm sweating like a boxer, working like a slave, fed like a bird, and treated like an animal. Why would I ask for a job change and get away from all that not to mention you."

"Girl, you is crazy." LilliePearl chortled.

Though I had a hard exterior, inside, I was anxious. Why was Classification paging me? I would soon find out.

"Sherral Kahey, you are being transferred from the line crew to Housekeeping under Msgt. Willis. You are to report to her on Monday morning," instructed the Classification officer in a monotone. She continued, "You are also being assigned a room on the first room. You will be in room 109B on Gemini 1.

"You are to report to the to the dorm control officer on Saturday morning after breakfast. Is all that understood?" she finished and took a breath as if she had said everything and was finished with me. I did not get the luxury of asking any questions or making any comments about my life. My life was "theirs". In the three months since intake, I'd learned a lot, but the most valuable lesson for me was learning to keep my mouth shut.

"Yes, Ma'am". Yes, I had learned my lesson well. With classification, there were no questions. You accepted whatever the change was to be. You have no life, no say-so, no input, no feedback, just "yes ma'am or yes sir". All decisions are made for you. There is no need to speak, think or express. All we had to do was wake up in the morning and the rest of the day was pre-planned for us. For some, it was a blessing not to have to make any decisions, not to have to be concerned about what to cook or what to eat. For me, It was a crippling disability that left me feeling as if I had re-visited childhood.

I was thrilled to be moving to a room as opposed to an open dormitory. Maybe I would be privy to a little more privacy. It was two long days until Saturday morning and I was eager to get to a room. My move to housekeeping was a less joyous one. Housekeeping was said to be a "set-up", because you were under the supervision of officers at all times. You had to stand and work at all times and if you had a restriction where you could not stand, you were allowed to sit, but you had to keep your hands moving at all times. My preference was to stay on the line crew where I had space and a job to do. Only thing is, I did not have the luxury of expressing a preference.

Saturday morning, I woke with such a feeling of enthusiasm that I had to check myself. I was excited about moving as if I were going to be moved out the institution. It was in the same building, just on another floor and in a room with a door and four walls. My state of exultation was due to the fact that I would have a little time to myself when I could look about and see that no one had me under surveillance.

After breakfast, there was an announcement for all inmates who had been re-classified to report to their assigned locations. When I reported to the officer, she said, "Why you coming to me? Didn't they give you a room number? Can't you read? The numbers are over the doors."

"Yes, Ma'am", I was a "good inmate, no comments, no grumbling, no back talk, but I was not broken or beaten, I was just wise.

"Then step to it," she commanded. I went down the hall glancing at the room numbers positioned over the doors. I also noticed that each room had two beds and an exposed clothes rack.

"*AH-HA*" I thought to myself. I had found 109.

"Hi there, Sherral" came the voice of the person inside the room sitting on one of the two bunk beds that was in the room. "Come on in here." This inmate had a thick Louisianan drawl.

"You have an advantage over me." I said, "You know my name, but I have not had the pleasure of meeting you."

Holding out a long, slender, chocolate hand, she said, "I'm Vera, Vera Lafourche."

I received her hand and said, "Hi, VeraVera Lafourche." We laughed at my attempt at humor. "Nice to meet you."

"This your bed, yeah." she pointed toward the bed opposite the one she was sitting on.

"That there is your rack for your clothes, "she continued, and this is our sink together. She said the word 'sink' as if it began with a "z".

That is when I knew, without asking that Vera was from New Orleans. The New Orleanians had a dialect all their own. Oil was "earl" Orange was "urnge"; sink was "zink"; all statements ended with, "yeah" or "yes, indeed". One went to "make grocery" instead of going to the grocery store. They called everyone they met "Boo". It was their term of endearment.

Every event was a reason to "celebrate". The women at this prison who were from New Orleans celebrated when someone was being released, they celebrated when someone they knew came to prison, they celebrated when someone was released from lockdown, they celebrated when someone went to lockdown. They celebrated when there was fried chicken on the menu. They celebrated when beans were served. They even celebrated when a new officer was hired, or an old one got fired or retired.

I knew that my stay in the room with Vera would be anything but boring. I wondered what lessons this person had for me to learn.

Vera was celebrating my becoming her roommate. She was bouncing around with the effervescence of a cheerful little girl. In fact, Vera was little. She was about 5'3". She looked to weigh about 90 pounds soaking wet, and she had very short, sandy hair that was neatly styled into a bob. Vera was a pretty female by anyone's standards, but she did not flaunt her assets as some I'd seen.

Vera was friendly. I wanted to know what she was in for, but as I stated, that was a taboo. You never inquired about another person's case. If they talked about it, that was different, if they never did, you just did not ask. As hyper as Vera was, I knew that in time, she would give me her entire life's story, charge included. Of course, there were a few souls who had the misfortune of having their cases posted in the Law Library. Those were the ones who had appealed their convictions. After the appeal was decided, the case was published for anyone to read. The disadvantage about that was that the case was biased in favor of the prosecution's arguments. Anyone who knew anything about the law knew that oft-times, the prosecutor sensationalized the case for publicity purposes. The truth was often distorted and then written as actual facts into law books. Reading the prosecutor's case made the offender look like "Public Enemy #1". Sometimes it was advantageous better to talk about your case before it reached the Supreme Court books. I watched as Vera acquainted me with "<u>our</u>" room.

"If you got a foot locker," she instructed, "it have to go under your bed."

"No," I replied, I don't have one right now, but I do plan to get one."

"Well, you gone need one for yo' food and "zoo-zoos". Zoo-zoos was prison-talk for chips, candy, cookies, gum, instant lunch, and other junk foods.

"If you ain't got yo' stuff locked, these rogues'll steal you blind," Vera warned.

"As soon as I get a little money in my account, I'll get one, although, I don't eat much junk food or sweets," I informed Vera, who just nodded her head as if to understand.

"Vera, "I began," I do one thing that might annoy you, and I hope it doesn't, but I do want to let you know out front."

"Naw, I'm easy to get along wiff," she remarked, "you can't get on my nerves or nothing' like that."

"You say that now, but later you might change," was my response, "anyway," I continued, "I pray in the morning and at noon and when I come in from work and then again at night."

"Is that all", Vera said.

"Yes." I answered.

"Hell, I might even join you in prayer", she interjected, "I like to pray to Jesus."

For months I had been at this facility and the only person faithfully practicing the Islamic faith. The only female wearing Islamic garments and Vera had not heard anything about me? I found that hard to believe.

"Have you had your head in the sand?" I asked Vera, playfully.

"What you mean?" she answered.

"I am a Muslim. I pray to God, but we refer to the Supreme Deity as "Allah" which is Arabic for God." I had no qualms about enlightening Vera.

"O-kay, just say 'God", then," she responded.

"Allah is God, and that is how I choose to refer to Him." I said. I did not want to get into a religious discussion with Vera or anyone else for that matter.

"What is the dorm officer's name?" I wanted to change the subject.

"Oh, she ain't nobody, her name is Sgt. Charbonet, Vera informed me, "She cool as a fan."

"I can't attest to how cool she is, but I do know that she is lazy," I said, just to keep the conversation going in another direction.

"Yeah, that what I mean when I say she cool", Vera schooled me, "she don't walk the halls so we can do anything we wants to do. Vera looked me straight in the face then, "you got a girlfriend?"

I said emphatically, "No, I don't and I am not looking for one either."

"Yeah-Yeah, that what they all say in the beginning," Vera mocked.

"Look, is there a certain time that I can wash my clothes", again I wanted this conversation to take another turn.

"It the same as it was upstairs where you jest came from", Vera sounded agitated. "Y'all all-time want to act like 'cause you done moved to another room or dorm or floor that you don't know the rules. Damn, it the same prison, with the same rules everywhere you go." Vera finished the statement and strutted from the room.

I guess she had gotten a little pissed at me by this time. I proceeded to settle myself into my new environment. As I unpacked, I noticed that several women passed my room and glanced in.

In an effort not to be rude, I did not get up and close the door, but I had a strong urge to be rude.

Just as I had finished unpacking, Vera entered the room with a "friend" that I could tell from first glance, that this female was a "homo" which in prison terms meant that she was an aggressive (male role) lesbian, and Vera's girlfriend.

"Sherral, this my girlfriend, Fred", Vera introduced us, "and Fred, this is my new roommate, Sherral."

"You play?" Fred spoke, harshly.

"Play what?" I asked innocently and sincerely. That response sparked uncontrolled laughter from Vera. Fred did not find it funny. Neither did I for that matter. I thought it was a legitimate question.

I stood there, the butt of a joke that Vera found funny beyond words. I felt like a fool as she continued to laugh. Fred smiled at her and just gave me a sneer.

I felt compelled to say something, "I play cards, but I don't gamble. I play volleyball and my favorite board game is Scrabble. I love to play Scrabble, and I was learning to play Bridge when I got this charge." I informed Fred. Vera was still in a waning state of laughter.

I wanted to make conversation, and this was my ineffectual attempt.

Vera recovered saying, "No, no, no, do you play house?"

I resisted the temptation to say I hadn't played house since I was twelve years old. I finally understood the gist of the conversation. Then, I was insulted, "Hell, no, I do not play with women, if that is what you mean by 'do I play'". Fred turned her back to me and said to Vera, "Bitch think she too good to be loved by a woman. A woman could make her feel better than any man ever could". I commented, boldly, "Matter of opinion." Then it dawned on me!

"Wait!" I was incredulous, "who are you calling a 'bitch! You have no right calling me anything other my name which is, Sherral."

Vera interrupted as she saw the course this verbal exchange was taking, "Look, uh Sherral, can you go in the game room for a while? Sgt. Charbonet will be gittin' off work in a while and I want to take advantage of the time."

"Leave the room? Why?" I questioned dumb-founded.

"Yeah, Miss Goodie-two-shoes," Fred affirmed, "git out!"

"The name is Sherral and what is your name, surely not Fred, I know your mother must have given you a beautiful feminine name." I was being deliberately off-handed. I was sick of being made to feel as if I were in the wrong. Fred advanced toward me. I stood where I was.

"Fred, I told you a thousand times, you can draw more flies wit honey than wit vinegar", Vera's sage advice meant nothing to Fred.

Fred responded, "ain't tryin to draw flies. I' m tryin to get rid of a pest."

"Fred, I asked you to keep your mouth shut and I would handle her", Vera was being the diplomat. *What did she mean by "handle me?" I thought.*

"I am not an animal to be handled or trained or dealt with," I felt my face go hot as I tried to control the sound of my voice. This was only my first day in this room and already there were problems.

"Look, Sherral, some of us do play and we play house if you know what I mean." Vera started explaining. I just sat on my bed listening to her as I grasped what she was saying.

Vera continued, "We hav'ta take care uh business when the opportunity come."

"And what does that have to do with me?" I wanted her to break it down for me although I had figured it out.

"If you want me, I can break it down for you." Vera sounded definite. "I know you ain't no nun and I know you ain't stupid. You been here four months and you know what go on in prison.

"And?" I was not giving in. I knew that I was making Vera uncomfortable. I also knew that I was getting on Fred's nerves. I regretted the former and gloated about the latter. Fred spoke up, "Oh, I know, you one of them freaks, you wanna watch, ain't no shame in my game, if Vera say you can, I'm game."

I was insulted. Fred had won that round. I paraded myself from the room and had the presence of mind to close the door behind me. I went to the TV area where there was constant noise. I could not understand how anyone could hear the television. The TV and game room were one large area. There was a Spades game going at one table; dominoes, at another table;

Dirty Hearts at another table and in the TV area, there were about three different conversations in progress as two females struggled to hear the Wheel of Fortune. I empathized and vowed never to frequent the game/TV area.

I noticed one female sitting in a chair in the TV area. It was obvious she was not interested in watching the program that was on the tv. Rather she was more interested in Sgt. Charbonet. It didn't take a rocket scientist or a "nun" to figure out that this person was on the lookout for my roommate and her girlfriend as they played house. I turned my back to her.

"Roomie, Roomie", I turned and spotted Vera standing in the hallway door that led down our hall. She was merrily beckoning for me.

"Yes, what do you want?" I asked.

"Come on," she directed me back to the room as if I were a child who had been dismissed for mama and daddy to take care of their business.

"Naw, Vera, I'm into Wheel of Fortune", I lied. I'll be down later".

"Whatever, but I rushed Fred so you could come back in the room, but that's the last time I do that," she sounded arrogant, as if I had done her an injustice.

"Fred, come on." Vera called down the hall. Fred emerged from the hall smiling and swaggering like a peacock. I could have easily smacked that grin 'round to the back of her neck!

Vera and Fred went to the Spades table and pulled up chairs to observe the game. Their "lookout" joined them.

I sat idly staring at the television and Vanna White. My thoughts went to my family. Robin loved Wheel of Fortune. I wondered if she was watching it now. I wondered it we were both viewing the same program. Saddened by that thought, and the thought that I would have to endure such conditions for what the judge said' the rest of my life, I felt a hot tear trickle down my face. I hurried to wipe the lone tear for fear someone would see me and get curious; or worse, someone would see it as a sign of weakness.

My subsequent thoughts were not much better; but they were more, "in-the-now". How long would I have to be in the room with Vera? How long would I have to put up with Fred? How long would I have to be incarcerated? The Judge had said "Life". I knew better than that? I rose from my seat; moved toward the door to retreat to my room.

"Sherral, you wanna play". There it was again, that word. This time Vera was asking me. How do I answer? I did not feel up to being the jester this time. In the end, I acted as if I had not heard the inquiry. I proceeded down the hall to the room I had been assigned. For some reason, I wanted to cry. I unpacked the rest of my belongings, took out my pajamas, gathered my shower supplies and went to the shower area down the hall. Once inside, I burst into a heart-wrenching cry.

The shower was the one place that a female could go to release the cares and woes of the day. The shower was the one place of privacy, odd as that seemed. Whenever I wanted to have a good cry, I'd spend time in the shower. There I would cry out and pour out my heart. I would talk, moan, groan and grieve. When I stepped from the shower, I felt better, ready to face another day, another challenge, another test, another day in the life behind bars and barbed wire. There are no rapes taking place in the shower. Contrary to what the media would have one believe, there are no weird-looking perverts lying in wait for a victim. The shower was one of my favorite places. It was the only place that you have to yourself. You don't share the shower stall with anyone. It's you, your thoughts, God, and your tears. Yes, in the shower, I could clear my body and cleanse my mind, purge myself of the stress and tension of the prison-day. It wasn't always that I cried, but there were times when I needed to get it out or go crazy. While many elected to do the latter, I chose the former. I was determined to return to society with a sound mind.

MOVIN' ON UP

"Sherral Kahey! Report to the Classification officer immediately", was the call from a feminine voice over the public announcement system.

"Here we go again. What is it now?" I thought to myself. Once more, I'd soon find out what plans classification had made for my life. What decisions had been made for me.

"You are on classification for a change in living area," Said a classification officer that I had not seen before. Administrative staff did not have to wear uniforms. This classification officer was dressed in clothes that I knew came from one of the finer women's clothiers. Her skin tone was a medium brown. Her hair and nails were well groomed, and her facial makeup was applied as if she had it done professionally just before she came to work. She was average height about 5'7" and from her seated position, I could tell that she was in good physical shape. Miss Classification Officer was a refreshing change from what I had come to know as the "norm".

"Yes, ma'am," I said, flatly.

"I'm Rhonda Bledsoe, your classification officer," Ms. Bledsoe said pleasantly. There are always at least two officers in classification; the other officer simply stared at me. No need for introductions, I knew that she was Assistant Warden of Security (AWS) Phyllis Troupe. She was in absolute contrast to Ms. Bledsoe. AWS Troupe was a short Caucasian woman with short salt-and-pepper hair that lay flatly to her head. Although she did not have to wear a uniform, AWS Troupe always wore one. I came to the conclusion that either she did not have many "civilian" outfits to wear or she was lazy and preferred wearing the worry-free, yet hot, double-knit uniform.

"You have been at the Louisiana Correctional Institute for Women for six months. No reports and no major difficulties. That speaks volumes for your behavior, and mental adjustment to confinement." said Ms. Bledsoe. I wondered where this was going. Did Ms. Bledsoe's declaration of my "behavior" mean that I had become institutionalized? I hoped not. Assistant Warden Troupe shifted uncomfortably in her chair.

In prison lingo, being "institutionalized" simply meant that one had conformed to the structure of the system and had relinquished her own mentality in lieu of the controlled environment of prison life. Basically, a person who was considered to be "institutionalized" had no mind of her own. The administrators in penal facilities can manage offenders better when the inmates are either drugged into a zombie state or "institutionalized". Neither state of being was cause for concern for the officers and administration.

Ms. Bledsoe continued, "You are being classified to Aquarius dormitory, C&F wing room C36. You are to report to the Dorm control officer in the Aquarius Rotunda after breakfast on Saturday morning. Take all your belongings because once you leave Gemini, you will need a pass to enter that area, do you understand?"

A pass was a sheet of paper that served as one's permission to enter what was called "restricted area" such as dormitories where one does not live, areas such as the library, cafeteria, and command areas. These places were off limits for inmates without that small sheet of paper that had been signed and issued by the dorm officer.

"Yes Ma'am." I replied. There was nothing else to say.

"You can go," was Assistant Warden Troupe's only contribution to the setting.

I exited the area and headed to my dorm. I had two days left in the room with Vera.

EXIT WOUNDS

"I knowed that as soon as I heard 'em pagin' you." Vera whined. She continued, "It don't never fail, soon as I git used to a roommate, she either go to lockdown, home, or to Aquarius."

"Well, I thought you would have been happy to be rid of me," I joked trying to lift Vera's mood.

"Naw, you the best roomie I done had in a long while. You stays to yourself, you don't talk a *whole* lot, but, gal, you can talk, you stays out me and my girl's way, you clean and you smart. I done learned a lot from you in two months."

"Thanks, Vera that was so nice of you to say."

Suddenly a shadow darkened our door. I looked and saw a tall boyish-looking Caucasian standing in our doorway.

"Come on Vee, you got me waiting out here." the boyish-girl said.

"Don't be rude, Bobby, speak to my roommate, Vera told the "girl-boy".

"Sherral," I said and offered her a hand to shake.

"Hi," she said, shaking my hand vigorously, "I'm Bobby Sawter, Vera told me about you." I wondered what Vera had told her about me.

"Sherral, Bobby is my new 'friend'" Vera didn't need to tell me that. She had introduced me to two other new 'friends' since Fred.

"Bobby, I ain't comin' back out there. I got to talk to Sherral. She movin' to Aquarius Saturday," Vera said.

"Okay, I'll be out in the game room if you wanna come out later," Bobby said as she exited the room. Vera turned a forlorn face toward me.

"Sherral, I'm gonna miss you, Girl. I ain't lying," Vera said in a whisper. I actually felt sorry for her.

"It isn't like I'm leaving the institution, Vera, I am only moving to another dorm. We will still be able to see each other."

"Girl, you get in that room with no other roommate and you got a key to the room and you can get a TV if you can afford one, and a boom box. You ain't comin' out. Then you don't even go to the kitchen, so when I'm a see you?"

"Vera, all you have to do is send for me and I will be out to see you." I said.

Vera wasn't being put off that easy, "Yeah, right."

"Come on now, you'll get a new roommate and forget all about me." I told her.

"I never get good roommates, you the best one I done had. You listen to me and you don't put me down and call me a "bull-dagger, and try to tell me about my "friends". Vera sounded almost on the verge of tears.

"Well, if it's any consolation, I'm going to miss you, Vera." I said sincerely. Suddenly, I felt like crying, as well.

One of the lessons that I learned is that one cannot afford to get too close to other offenders. Something was always happening to them. They went home, they went to lockdown, they changed jobs, changed rooms, they took lovers who alienated them from other friends. There was always something to separate friendships

I totally understood what Vera was saying and what she was experiencing. She had bonded with me over the months that we had been roommates, now I was moving to another area.

I made up in my mind that my friends would be ones that had time to be at the facility. That way I would not have to deal with the pain of having someone leave me behind. Over the months that I had been at the Louisiana Correctional Institute for Women, I had met a lot of people, I had worked with offenders, but I had not allowed anyone to get close to me. Vera and I had come as close to bonding as any two people could. She and I share space and time. We had gotten to know each other relatively well. She had a few months left to serve and she would have been leaving me anyway. I felt a twinge of sadness as I realized that I would not be her roommate anymore. Then, once she left the confines of this facility, I would not see her again in life.

Vera was not a person I thought would come back to prison. On that point, I hoped that I would not see her again, not in here, at least. How oddly sobering that inmates are forced to live with individuals we had never seen before, individuals who are quite different from each other, individuals with different backgrounds, cultures, nationalities, morals, and beliefs, and once thrust together, we learn to accept or at least to tolerate each other. In the worst case scenario some roommates hate each other. We have no choice of who would be our roommates so it was up to us to make the best of the situation. Usually, this is done by getting to know each other, respect each other and mostly to ignore petty differences, prejudices and personal judgments that only create more problems than solutions.

As much as I wanted to live in Aquarius, and as much as I wanted my own small space, I was sad that the first person that I had been forced to bond with was on her way out of my life.

"Vera, nothing lasts forever", I had to change the tone of this exchange, "when I came in this room, we knew that one of us would leave the other, right?"

"Yeah", Vera agreed, "but I wanted to leave you in this room. I thought you woulda been here until I left."

That statement from Vera posed another question in my mind, "Vera, do you think that a person with a life sentence will die in prison?"

Vera looked at me as if I had asked her to cut her throat. Then, "Well, I ain't seen no lifer leave here unless she escaped," Vera replied. "I been here seven years and I ain't seen no lifers leave, 'cept over the fence."

"Vera, I plan to leave here and I plan to walk out the front gate the same way I walked in here." I exclaimed. My cheeks burned as I continued, "to live and die in prison is not my destiny, Vera, and I plan to have a life back in society one day."

"Well," Vera said after a moment's thought, "I guess all lifers feel like that, but like I said, I ain't seen none leave here the right way like you saying."

"I will!" were the last words I had to add to that conversation.

Lifers had no hope of release according to the policies and procedures of the department of corrections. There was some truth to what the judge said, "without benefit of probation, parole or suspension of sentence." With lifers, the only hope was slim at best. Our only recourse other than re-entering the court system, was the pardon board.

Pardon Boards seldom gave lifers a chance to be free. Lifers essentially had no hope. The prison population was cognitive of that fact.

As I pondered this particular train of thought, a series of statements played in my head. The words I had heard so often when a lifer would get into an argument with another offender. They were words that cut to the bone marrow of a female offender sentences to life:

"Life doin' Bitch"

"You gonna die here with that life sentence you got!"

"You gone be here when the bricks fall, with that life sentence!"

"Only way you gonna leave is in a black body bag."

"Yeah, you'll be here when I git back."

"This your home, B"

"When you see society again, they gonna be driving space ships on the streets!"

"I'm goin home, but you ain't goin nowhere wit that life sentence you got."

They were cruel, mean, razor-sharp words spoken in anger to wound a lifer, to drive home the fact that a lifer had no hope and that was an accepted fact. It was also a fact that I would not, could not allow myself to consider or accept. The days from Thursday to Saturday were a blurred mixture of emotions for Vera and me. Finally, it was Saturday morning, moving day. Vera skipped breakfast which was unheard of for her. She was petite, but she ate like a big woman.

Vera said, "I slept through breakfast! I ain't heard 'em even call it"

"I thought you wanted to sleep, so I didn't wake you", I said.

"I guess you all packed, huh?" Vera looked at the bags and boxes all over the floor.

"Yeah, I finished packing this morning after my prayer time." I explained. "I hope I didn't wake you, but I guess not since you missed breakfast. Look, if you are hungry, I have some instant oatmeal. You are welcomed to it."

"Naw, I ain't got no appetite." Vera mumbled. As petite as Vera was, she seemed to have shrunk about two inches in height. My heart felt so heavy.

There was a deep sadness that hovered in our room. I actually wanted to cry and I could not shake the feeling. Vera looked so sad. I knew that I would miss her as much as she would miss me. I thought of an old saying, I think about a line from a movie or play or something like that, *"Parting is such sweet sorrow."* I could not relate to the "sweet" but the sorrow was apparent in both our expressions.

"All residents who have been classified to move may now do so," came the announcement over the public announcement system. That broke the silence, and opened the door to our final moments as roommates. Vera began to cry.

"Aw, Vera, don't do that, you will be just fine and I'll make a point of seeing you every day."

Vera did not reply. She walked over to my packed belongings, hoisted a huge bundle over her shoulders and walked out the room, still crying. I followed suit and grabbed another bundle. Bobby seemed to come from nowhere and grabbed two bundles, one over each shoulder, "show-off". I smiled and made a mental calculation that women were expected to do men's work yet keep their femininity. I thought, *now that is an oxymoron if I ever heard one.*

"Damn, Sherral you show did accumulate a lot of stuff since you been here!" chimed Bobby.

"Shut up and help!" growled Vera.

We walked the rest of the way to Aquarius in silence. At least, Vera had stopped crying. I was glad to see that. My heart was hurting as well. Once in front of Aquarius dormitory, Vera and Bobby had to put my belongings on the ground because they were not allowed to proceed inside the building, much less to my new domain. There was a tall, stern-looking officer standing in front of the dorm to make sure that only the designated persons entered the building.

"Who is the one moving to this dorm?" the officer asked.

"I am." I simply replied.

Vera and I looked at each other. It was a rule violation for us to hug, which would have been the normal thing to do, but nothing about prison was "normal".

Then, "Sherral, you left your plants in my room," Vera said, suddenly and urgently. I was puzzled because I did not have any plants. Suddenly, it dawned on me. I complied.

"Okay, I'll go get them," I said.

"Bobby, you stay here wit her stuff while we go git her plants." Vera ordered.

We walked back to my old dorm as if we were really headed that way to collect plants. It was funny. We both started laughing. Once inside Gemini, we went to what was once our room. Inside the door, Vera and I embraced. We said nothing for there was nothing to say, but it felt comforting to have that human touch that is vital and necessary to the process of connecting and bonding with each other. It wasn't a perverted hug in any way or stretch of the imagination. It was the embrace of two females who shared so much more than a space. It was the embrace of two females who needed to belong to something more than a penal facility. It was the embrace of two people who had grown together and were now being torn apart, not of our own doing which hurt even worse. The embrace was only for a few seconds, but it seemed much longer, and it felt naturally, normally and expectedly good. It was disheartening to realize that such a natural act would have landed us in lockdown if an officer had seen the embrace. Even in the comfort of the act, there was also the tension, fear of getting caught. Vera did not cry as I suspected she would, but there was such a cloud of sadness. "Exit *wounds*" was the only word that came to mind. After releasing the embrace, I exited, the room that Vera and I had shared. We walked to Aquarius in silence once more, both our heads down, eyes filled with tears that we could not allow anyone to see.

"Where the plants?" the officer at the dorm of Aquarius asked.

"I decided to leave them in the room." I lied. Lying was something that I did not enjoy doing, but another lesson in life inside. Lying was a way of life. The officers never believed anything an offender said unless it was something that was spoken against another offender. Usually they were correct not to believe us because the system was set up in a manner that forced offenders to lie about the smallest, most insignificant things.

Rules and regulations were instituted to create lying. If a fellow offender were hungry, it was a rule infraction for me to give her something to eat. If someone needed soap and I gave her a bar of soap, I was in violation of a rule. If a friend had a death in her family, I had to stand at a 'safe' distance and watch her cry without so much as a pat on the shoulder, a hug or even an offer to hold her hand to comfort her. Then, if she cried too much, she was placed on protective custody. Protective Custody is an administrative term for locking one in an isolation cell for protective reasons, either from oneself or from others. When a person has had a death in her family, the last thing she needed was to be locked away from her associates. To get beyond these rules, we learn to lie. What a system of "correction".

I carried my belongings into my new living area without help from the offenders that were sitting in front of the dorm. Once I checked into the dorm control, got my room number and door key, I proceeded to my newly assigned single room. The thought of Vera tugged at my heart. She was such a sweet person. She had grown so attached to me in such a short time. In fact, I felt as if she were one of my children. There were also times that Vera would say that I reminded her of her mother, except I wasn't an alcoholic. Her mother was an alcoholic who, as Vera said, became abusive when she drank. Guess who was the recipient of the abuse? Vera was the only child that the Office of Child Services (OCS) had not taken from her mother. She said she had four brothers and a sister that she had no idea where they were. She never knew why she wasn't taken. Vera said that she thought they left her with her mother so that her mother would have someone to beat up on. Although, I told her that that was absurd, I also wondered why they had not taken Vera. Vera was yet another victim who had fallen through the cracks of our imperfect social system.

BIG HOUSE-LITTLE ANGOLA

Aquarius was a huge building that had three wing and six tiers, two tiers per wing. It was referred to as the "Big House" because it was the largest building on the compound. Both the buildings were named after the Zodiac signs of employers, for example, *Gemini* was named for the current warden. *Aquarius* was named for the oldest security officer at the facility at the time, Captain Della Jasper. Captain Jasper was a petite woman who stood about 5'3" tall. She was somewhat on the chubby side, but she camouflaged her weight by wearing tight uniforms that fit like a girdle making her appear to be smaller than her weight indicated. Her hair was dyed auburn and she wore heavy makeup which made Capt. Jasper look hard. I believe that she wore the heavy make-up deliberately to compensate for her small stature and to intimidate the offenders into submission. It worked because Captain Delia Jasper was the most feared officer on the compound, which included the men that worked there. Captain Jasper had been in corrections for 22 years making her the oldest black correctional officer in the state. In reference to "oldest", this was not in years, but in time spent in the penal system.

The wings in Aquarius were alphabetical. The wing on the right as you entered the rotunda of the building was A & D wing, the former being the lower level and the latter was the upstairs wing. C & F Wing was to the left and across from A &D. Wing B & E was straight and to the rear of the building as you entered the rotunda.

There were also two isolations wings diagonally located between A&D and B&E. This isolation area was used as lockdown for the worst-acting, most uncontrollable offenders. One cell was padded.

I was moved to the wing that was called, "Little Angola", which was C & F wing. I had a room on the lower level or C-wing. The wing earned its name because it housed the repeat offenders, the hardened criminals, and the lifers. These were the ones who were considered to be the worst of all the offenders. The ones who were considered hopeless criminals: the con-artists, the manipulators, the ones who were the least trusted and most feared by administration. As I headed to my room, I saw eyes on me. I was used to that by now, so I wasn't daunted by their stares, their whispers, or their snickers. The snickers usually came as a result of my wearing apparel; the whispers where because of my charge and the stares were because I was different. They didn't know what to make of me.

Six months it had taken me to get to this level. This was the next best thing to actually being "free". I had my own room, my own key to my room. I had a door that I could close and detach myself from the whispers, stares and snickers. I could be alone, finally. No, I wasn't free, but I surely felt free.

I spent most of the morning cleaning my room which also had a sink and toilet in it. My bunk style bed was across from the sink and toilet area. There was a long narrow window that looked out onto the grounds of the institution. The landscaping was immaculate. There was a standup locker that was the closet area for my clothes. The closet had a shelf at the top that I used for my food supplies. Beside the bunk bed was a small night stand with three drawers. The previous occupant had not been very clean. The room spelled strongly of cigarette smoke, urine and body odor. Working in housekeeping had its "fringed benefits". I had access to cleaning supplies that I used to clean, sterilize and deodorize the room.

In the late afternoon following the noon head count, there was a knock at my door. The door had a small 6x6 window primarily for security purposes. I looked out the window to see a familiar face. It was the person I had seen upon my intake in the Library, Billy. Her face covered the window. For a brief moment, I was frightened, in spite of the emotion, I turned the knob and opened the door.

"Billy, hi," I said calmly, as if we were old friends.

"Oh, so you remembered my name," said Billy, flattered. I wondered if I had given her the wrong impression by remembering her name. I surely did not want her to think anything other than the fact that she had been helpful to me at a low point in my intake process.

"Yes, I appreciated your words of encouragement. They helped me make it through the rest of that day." I admitted.

"Well, I'm right next door to you on the left, so if you need anything let me know." she said.

"Thanks, Billy, I'll remember that." I commented. I had no intention of "needing" anything from Billy or from anyone else for that matter. One lesson learned in prison: *Everyone had a motive for being nice.* Nothing comes free or easy in the penal environment. There was a price attached to everything. I had hoped that I wasn't becoming paranoid, but I wasn't taking any chances.

Six months inside and it felt like I had been incarcerated for six years, yet at the same time, it felt as if I had just arrived. Truthfully, I did not know how long I would be at LCIW, but I knew from the beginning that this place was not my end. There was a reason for my being at this facility and it had little or nothing to do with what the court had done. It had nothing to do with my committing a crime. I felt then as I did throughout my time that there was a reason beyond what my eyes could see or my mind could conceive.

Yes, this was the wing they called, "Little Angola". Everyone on these wings, C &F, was either a lifer or a repeat offender with double digits time, ten or more years. Most of the double digits were numbers like 20, 40 and 99 years. For the most part, the offenders were murderers, female victims of domestic violence; or drug users of heroin or armed robbers who robbed to support their drug habits. These were the "hardened criminals".

The first full morning, in my room, with my door closed, I stayed up following the early morning 4:45 a.m. count, did my ablution and said my prayer. I sat on my bed and read from my Qu-ran until a soft knock came at my door ending my peaceful moments. I went to the door. There was a tall, slender grey-haired female standing on the outside of my door. As I opened the door, this lady shoved two boxes of single serving raisin bran cereal and two cartons of mild in my hands. "Here," she said, "I heard that you don't go to the kitchen. My name is Annie, but everybody calls me Granny." Then she left my door. It happened so suddenly it caught me totally by surprise. I didn't know what to say. I stood there in the door watching this lady go down the hall and disappear from my sight. I hid the cereal and milk in my locker because it was a rule violation to have food from the kitchen in our possession outside the cafeteria.

Honestly, I was grateful for Granny's gesture, yet at the same time, I wondered what she wanted for this food. I knew that kitchen workers sold food from the cafeteria as a means of "self-support"; a hustle is what it was called. I did not have any money to pay for food. I had money on my prison account called a 'book', but that was not much at all. My sister and grandmother would sent me a few dollars once a month or so. I refused to ask them for money because they were the caretakers for my five children. How could I burden them by asking for money? No, I had made up my mind to get by as best I could. But back to Granny, I was confused about what to do about this current turn of events. I decided to do nothing for the time being. I only ate once a day and that was in the later afternoon about 5 o'clock. I had time to see Granny and clarify the situation. After the noon count, there came another knock at my door. I opened it to find Billy standing there.

"Sherral, mind if I come in for a minute?" she asked. I was instantly nervous, but I played it off.

"Sure Billy, come on in." I invited.

"Look, I ain't tryin' to be in your business or nothing like that but in here word gets around like really fast, so everybody know you don't go to the kitchen to eat 'cause of your religion and you don't eat poke so I brung you some stuff. She reached under her blouse and came out with three boiled eggs. She reached in her pants pockets and produced in one hand a tomato and in the other an onion.

"No, thanks Billy but I can't take this stuff. Really, I appreciate it, but I'll be alright. Thanks, anyway though." I was appreciative but I did not understand the gesture which made me feel uneasy.

Billy walked past me and put the items on the nightstand saying, "Ain't no time for being proud in prison. You gone get pretty hungry if all you eat come out the canteen."

"Billy, I can manage, really, I am fine," I said.

"Well, you can throw that stuff away, but I ain't takin' it outta here." Billy said, and left my room.

There was sincerity in these two acts of kindness. These females had taken food from the cafeteria, risked getting caught and getting a rule infraction, brought the items to me and had not asked for anything in return, yet. I began to wonder if these people had brought the food to me to set me up. Why? What would make them want to set me up? What should I do with this food? Would the next knock at my door be officers coming to shake my room and find the food? Was I being paranoid? Or was I being cautious? If I erred, I would rather err on the side of caution. I put the cereal, milk, eggs, tomato and onion in a brown bag to conceal them in case I ran into Billy or Granny on the way to the garbage can. I tossed the bag in the can and walked away, feeling really guilty for throwing the food away.

The rest of my day was uneventful. I stayed in my room all day and enjoyed the solitude. In the evening I went to my locker, retrieved a can of sardines and a pack of crackers. As I opened the can and poured the contents in a bowl, I couldn't help thinking how good the meal would have been with the items I had trashed. After all, as I said, the rest of my day was uneventful therefore; no officers came to my room. Neither Billy nor Granny had come to me for "payment", either. I shook my head realizing that I had made a mistake. Was I becoming paranoid? It was too early in my sentence for that type of mentality.

My room was in front of the game room and the tv area. The game room was on a split level sunken floor that held six card tables with four chairs at each table. There was usually a couple of card games taking place and as many domino games. Both games, cards and dominoes, were noisy. The cards were always being popped and slammed on the card table. The players were talking loudly, bluffing each other and cursing. The dominoes were noisy because the players slammed them on the table and shuffled them noisily on the table. They, as well, did a lot of loud talking and cursing, all in the name of fun. I didn't need my door opened to hear the dialog that took place between the players. I could hear everything loudly and clearly. One good thing about me, noise did not bother me the way that it did some of the females.

"You, Bitches, ain't got no 'spect for nobody!" Yelled my neighbor across the hall. Her name was Ellafaye.

"Ol' Hag, put cotton in your ears", replied one of the card players, "you ain't in no nursing home. This the pen, and we playin Spades, havin' fun and you jest mad."

"Ho, I ain't no hag but yo' maw is!" responded Ellafaye.

The card player threw the cards she had in her hand at my neighbor who crayfished back into her room. The card player ran to Ellafaye's door and peered into the small window while she banged on the door with her fist. "You piece a trash, you don't talk 'bout my mama, you bitch you. Open this door and I'll show you who is the hag."

By this time the dormitory security officers are on the wing and advancing toward the card player.

An officer commanded," Paulette, you have a direct order to stop beating on that door!"

Paulette stopped immediately, but was still yelling, "She don't talk 'bout my mama and git away wit it."

"What you gonna do, huh? You plan on goin' in there on her and whipping her ass?" said the officer that accompanied the first one.

"Naw, you don't play me like that, Sgt. Theriot. You ain't fix ta lock me up on the funny style," said Paulette.

"What funny style, Convict, if I wanted to, I could lock you up right now for banging on that door, That is an act of aggression," blurted the second officer.

Ellafaye appeared at her door, "Officer Theriot, all I said was they was makin' too much noise with that Spade game."

"Shut up, Convict, ain't nobody talking to you, YET!" spat the first officer. I could not see Ellafaye's face, but I could almost feel the heat from it through the walls. She had been angered, embarrassed and humiliated in a matter of minutes. It didn't matter that her claim had merit. It didn't matter that there was an excessive amount of noise coming from bother the card games and the domino games. It also did not matter that Ellafaye was in the right. Although her grievance had merit, she was threatened as if she had been in the wrong. As I evaluated the situation I realized that all of us were "in the wrong" simply because we were convicts.

Here I was situated between two of the noisiest places on the compound. There would not be a dull or quiet moment. For a certainty, I was in for some serious mental adjusting if my intentions were to maintain my sanity and peace of mind. I knew that I would have to modify my thought process in order to tune out noise. I knew that I had to find a place within myself that nullified me to the outer disturbances. There were a couple of phrases added to the list of "common convict statements". *"This ain't no rest home!"* and, *"You ain't at home!"* I could surely attest to both declarations.

LEARNING THE ROPES

My money was running out. I had spent wisely and made the money I had come to the institution with last, but now I was out of money. The facts were before me: I was a Muslim; I was serving a life sentence; I did not have any more money, and I did not eat pork. So far, I had managed to stay out the institution's cafeteria with the help of the kind-hearted inmates who would bring me food items I could eat from the kitchen. I also budgeted the money I had come to the facility with. How was I going to survive in this penal facility working on the line crew, in the heat of summer, wearing my traditional Islamic attire, and adhering to the Islamic dietary guidelines? This situation was ingredients for disaster. I needed an income. I could not nor would not solicit my family for money each month. They were caring for my five children without assistance from other family members. Asking my husband's family to assist was futile.

Coming from a proud family of Native American and Irish ancestors, we were not raised to take "charity" from city, state or government programs designed to help the needy. I knew that my sister would not apply for assistance of any type. She would struggle along with nine children and as my great-aunt would say, "make do or do without". As children we did without more often than we made do. Yet, we learned some valuable life lessons from our struggle and I was certain that my sister would apply those lessons in her current situation.

My religious practices prohibited me from eating meals in the "pork infested" cafeteria. I could not depend on other inmates to steal food for me, nor would I ask anyone to violate the rules for me. It was one thing for me to violate, but I would not ask another person to do it. What was I to do? Yes, I could go to the cafeteria, but being the stubborn and devout Muslim that I was, I had to find a way out of this situation without violating my religious rules and without violating the institutions rules.

This institution did not have any provisions for people who did not eat pork. My first decision was to go to the Law Library and do some research on the issues and where I stood. Surprisingly, I learned that most other institutions did indeed have requirements for Muslims who did not eat pork. Immediately, I decided to request a non-pork diet for myself and for any other Muslims who were adhering to the Islamic diet.

I wrote a letter to the warden formally making my request for provisions for Muslims. I was specific in what was needed and expressed my desire that these needs be met without delay. The letter fell upon deaf ears resulting in a flat denial. I had not anticipated a negative response, but I understood the rejection coming from this warden.

Warden Freddy Franklin was an African-American man who stood about 5'7" with his shoes on. He had a supercilious attitude and disposition. His skin was dark brown and ruddy-looking; he had a thick mustache and a goatee. His eyes were dark brown, small and beady. He was constantly shifting them from side-to-side as if to spot anyone who might attempt to sneak up on him. He usually wore razor-creased, starched designer jeans, a crispy pressed long-sleeved shirt year-round, and a Stetson hat that covered his balding head. Warden Franklin looked to be about 40 something. He was a man of slight build but his frame looked fit for a man his age. He was bow-legged so many of the females (inmates and staff) considered him a "hunk". I didn't share their opinion of him but hunk, like beauty is in the eye of the beholder. Warden Franklin would walk the compound about once each day. He would talk to the women and sometimes he would cavort with the repeat offenders because he knew them relatively well. Of course, Carlass fit in that category. She loved it when the warden would call her by name and ask her, "Carlass, where did you stash the dope you brought in my facility?" The other inmates would chuckle uncontrollably as if that was the funniest thing they had ever heard. The irony is that he said it all the time, all he did was put another name to the question. How was the same joke funny the thousandth time? This arrogant warden had denied me something that I knew by law of the United States Constitution; I had a right to receive.

My next step was to file a federal lawsuit because my Fifth Amendment Rights to exercise my religious practices was being violated. But I also knew that the lawsuit would take years. I had to do something in the meantime or starve to death which was not my plan. As I appraised my current situation, I remembered that I had seen the shelves in the visiting room where inmates sold their wares. I decided that the craft idea was worth my investigating. I knew how to sew, but I had left my Singer behind. I would have to use some of my limited resources to purchase a machine. Maybe I could make things to sell in the visitation area. At least that would be a way that I could sustain myself without taxing my over-burdened family.

I came to LCIW with about $195.00. I knew that being a new commit I was not eligible for having a sewing machine. An inmate had to be a blue card holder in order to earn the privilege of having a sewing machine along with a color TV, and a cassette player.

There were three custody statuses. When a female entered the facility as a new commit, she was issued an orange card with her name and DOC number typed on it. That card indicated to the officers and other administrative personnel that the offender was limited in what she could do, where she could work, how long she was allowed to stay up at night and how many phone calls she could make per month. Orange card holders were at the bottom of the totem pole. Those brandishing the orange card were not privy to anything beyond the bare necessities and no privileges. Orange card holders got the worst jobs, worked hardest for the least amount-no earnings-and limited benefits. They were allowed to make two calls per month. They were allowed to have one visit per month, and they could not receive any outside packages. Outside packages had to be mailed from a mail-order company and were subject to search and denial of the package if the circumstances surrounding the package were suspect. No food items were allowed except at Christmas time.

The next status was the red card holders. This card was for females who were working to earn more privileges than the lower-level orange card holders. The red card holders were usually re-classified from the line crew, housekeeping and kitchen soon after earning the new status. They were moved to the honor dorm with the understanding that they would continue to strive for honor status. The red card holders were able to make one call per week. They were allowed two visits per month and they could receive one outside package per month. Their job assignments were less manual and demanding. Usually the red card holders worked in the gym, on the floor duties, or on the inner yard detail.

The third status was the highest which was the blue card holder. Those donning the blue cards were the envied and honor residents.

They had coveted privileges and positions. These female offenders had earned the privilege to stay up until midnight on week-ends, they had eight calls per month, they could receive two packages per month plus one hobby craft, in the summer they could have a picnic with their families. They held the better jobs such as tutors, library workers, counsel substitutes, office clerks and infirmary orderlies. They could have a color TV, cassette player, and a sewing machine as well as other hobby craft paraphernalia. Everyone wanted the privileges of being a blue card holder but not everyone made it to that level because of all the rhetoric one had to swallow in order to earn the blue card. When an inmate wore a blue card, you knew she had earned it. The main thing was to stay report-free. Disciplinary infractions were the basis of one's custody status. More than two disciplinary reports would bust an inmate back to the orange card status. If a blue card holder got busted down to orange card, she had to mail all her appliances home. At any rate my orange card limited me to how I could make extra money.

One Saturday morning I saw a female in the game room. She had a skein of yarn and she was crocheting something. I watched her in amazement as she quietly and peacefully went about her crocheting. She seemed to be in another world, she appeared so serene that just my observing her made me calm. Her name was Portia. She was a blue card holder. Portia was short and dumpy about 4 feet tall. She was also a blue card holder and she was one of three offenders who worked cleaning the visitation room each mornings and evenings. I had seen her several times but had not spoken to her. I walked from my door to the table where she sat. "Good morning, Portia", I said as I approached.

She didn't look up; she nodded her head in response to my greeting.

"What are you crocheting?" I inquired.

"I come down here to work not talk, and I can't talk when I'm counting," was her retort.

"Sorry. I was just curious." I said as I retreated to my room. Portia may have seemed calm but her disposition was anything but calm.

"Anyway, I don't befriend no baby killers", she added as I reached my door.

I was shocked at her outburst, "I don't blame you, I wouldn't either", was all I could think of to say back to her.

I continued to glance out my window at Portia because I was curious about what that ball of yarn would produce. Hours later, to my surprise, there was a beautifully crafted poodle tissue cover on the table where Portia sat. It amazed me that she had taken a skein of yarn and constructed such an adorable item. There was about a third of the yarn left. Several inmates gathered around to see the item and then an officer came to the table.

"Portia, you through with my poodle, I don't want all these inmates handling my stuff or I won't buy it", commanded the officer.

"Ain't no inmates handling your stuff, and you gone buy it cause we done already did the contract", Portia smarted off to the officer.

From that conversation I later learned that officers could purchase hobby craft items from inmates. There was a contract that had to be completed, signed by both parties and approved by about three other officials including the warden. The contract was legal and binding. The warden would not allow security officers or other staff members to violate a contract that was signed. The selling of hobby craft was one way that the inmates could have a little money placed in their accounts. It was a way of sustaining oneself without calling home for money, stealing from other inmates, or begging other inmates for what they had. I knew that I needed to learn to crochet, but who would teach me. I was reluctant to approach anyone; I usually waited for them to address me. Remarks like what Portia said to me made me leery of people. Portia had shocked me and hurt my feelings so I did not want to set myself up for any other such confrontations.

The following morning, Sunday, there was a light knock at my door. I knew it wasn't security officers wanting to shakedown officers knocked hard and entered the room simultaneously. I went to the door to see a Caucasian standing there. She had honey-blond hair, blue-gray eyes, very light freckles on her face, long eyelashes, somewhat thin without being skinny, and she smiled as I opened the door.

"Hi, Tamara Dobbson," said as if I should have recognized the name.

"And, I'm Sherral, so what now". Caucasians weren't my favorite ethnic group, needless to say.

"Well, I was at the water fountain yesterday and I heard the verbal exchange between you and Portia," Tamara added.

"So you came to offer your condolence?" I was being sarcastic as a defense mechanism for my embarrassment.

"No, I came to offer my help. Portia makes those tissue covers and she is making a killing on them, plus she does second rate work. She will not give the pattern to anyone and she is going home next month". I stepped aside and Tamara entered my room. "I heard that you were looking to make some extra money and I know you don't eat from the cafeteria. I had an idea", Tamara looked at me for a response.

"Why?" I asked, baffled at her knowledge and her offer.

"Well, Sherral, it's like this, I didn't like the way Portia addressed you in front of all the game room and really, I don't like Portia. She is a mean, ugly, nasty convict except to the cops!" Tamara educated me.

"Do you know how to crochet?" she asked.

"No", I replied.

"You have any yarn, hooks, and other stuff like that?" she continued.

"No", I answered.

"You have any kind of books, magazines, or anything that has crochet patterns in it?" Tamara inquired.

"No", I replied for the third time.

"Well, I'll tell you what, here's what I'll do. I have several hooks, and I keep extra yarn in my locker. You come to my room tomorrow after supper and I'll teach you to crochet", Tamara said, then "if you want me to and if that fits with your schedule. I don't mean to be pushy or demanding, I'm sorry".

Once again, the question popped into my head, "Why", but this time I did not verbalize. I was perplexed. I was also cautious because everyone in prison does something for something.

"Thanks, Tamara, I don't go to supper so when would you like for me to come and what is your room number?" I asked.

"I'm on the center hall room C-28. I don't go to supper either so you can come right after the 4:15 count. Is that a good time for you?" she added.

"No, but I can come at 5:15, if that is a good time for you", I said. I didn't want to get into my religious rituals, but I had a prayer at 5:00 p.m. every evening.

"Okay, I'll see you then", Tamara said as she prepared to exit my domain.

After Tamara left, I sat on my bed for a while thinking about what had just happened. This Caucasian that I did not know had freely offered her services. What was she expecting from me? I was fast turning into a paranoid person, suspicious of everyone and their motives. Well, if I was going to crochet, then I would eventually need my own supplies, books and patterns.

Tamara was true to her word. We met in her room about three times a week so that she could teach me the basics of crochet. She also had a color television that I really enjoyed watching. Tamara was patient with me and taught me the different stitches and how to read a pattern. One evening I told Tamara that I wanted to learn to make the poodle tissue cover that Portia was making.

"She's about to leave LCIW and I'll wait until after she leaves to make them," I said.

"I'll tell you what I can do. I'll buy one from her and we can take it loose and see how it's made. You can write as I take it apart and see what stitches and how many are used," Tamara said. That is what she did and what I did and that is how I began supporting myself in prison.

Tamara Dobbson, at the time, was the only female on the compound who had been on death row. Her sentence was commuted to a life sentence when the United States Supreme Court ruled the death penalty unconstitutional. She had gone from death row, to a life sentence, to a commutation of her sentence, and finally to freedom.

I learned all the basic stitches. I learned to read patterns and I began making items that were placed in the visiting room. There was money coming in for me, not on a regular basis, but it was always there when I needed it. It would seem that I was down to my last penny and all of a sudden, there would be a money slip where someone had bought one of my poodle tissue covers from the visiting room. Sometimes I received money from home, but I never asked. It was never a large amount, but I appreciated what they could and did send. I was able to take care of myself and that made me feel really good about myself even in this devastating, dehumanizing, degrading position that I found myself in.

CHANGES

Seconds, minutes, hours, days weeks and months melted into what was the days of my life. The days were the same. I learned to keep track of the days by what was served in the institution's cafeteria. Although I didn't go there, the meals were the second main event of the day in the life of incarcerated individuals, mail call being the first. Lunch was the biggest meal of the day. After lunch, everyone waited for mail call hoping to be the recipient of a receipt for money that was placed into your account, or pictures and news from home and if you were special, you received both. The lunch meal was as follows: Mondays was beef stew and rice for lunch. Tuesdays was red beans and rice; Wednesdays we were served chicken: fried, baked, stewed, smothered or my favorite-chicken salad. Thursday was meat sauce and spaghetti; and of course Fridays was always fish either fried fish, always catfish and there were times when tuna was served in various dishes or casseroles.

One weekend evening on the few occasions when my door was opened, I was sitting on my bed with my back to the door; a voice penetrated my ears, "Is that your hair?" I turned to see an attractive woman standing just outside my door in the hallway. I'd seen her but I didn't know her name.

"Yes, it is", I answered her, politely.

"I thought you were bald-headed." She said flatly. "Why do you hide such long beautiful hair? If I had hair like that, it sho' wouldn't be under no head rag."

"Well, Sister, I am not hiding my hair. I am covering it. I am Muslim and covering my hair is appropriate in public. When in the privacy of my home, or in this case, my room, I may relax my head dress. The reason I cover my hair and by body is because my beauty is only for my husband to observe", I explained, calmly. Then to lighten the moment, I added, "There's an adage that says, 'There is mystery in what is hidden.'" I gave this sister a kind smile indicating I did not mind her curiousness.

"I'm sorry. My name is Willie Mae. I know your name is Sherral, but I have never seen such beautiful coal black hair and I just didn't know yours was so long and pretty. It shocked me when I passed and seen it. I had to backup and do a double take."

"That's okay. I'm used to that reaction when people see me without my head covered", I said, "and it is nice meeting you, Willie Mae". I truly meant those words. I felt we were kindred spirits. There was an instant connection that I did not understand. I wondered what was the connect with this sweet and frank lady. I liked her instantly.

"I heard a little 'bout Muslims but I'ma tell you the truth, I don't know much 'bout it and don't wanna neither. I'ma borned-again Christian and it's all about Jesus in my life. All I want to know is JESUS", Willie Mae declared matter-of-factly. Usually that statement or others like it were red flags for me, indicating to me that I was to beware and stay clear of these types of people. In my experiences as a Muslim, I had witnessed and experienced countless 'Christians' whose main mission in life was to convert Muslims into Christians. Yet no mental red flags had gone up. For the second time since meeting Willie Mae, I was perplexed about her impact on me, or rather my lack of caution toward her. She was definitely different.

"My room is C-23 on the center hall. You can come down there anytime you want to," she invited peacefully. Willie Mae had such calmness about her that I accepted her invitation before I could stop myself.

"I'll do that some time," I replied.

"Come on now, ain't no time like the present. We can talk without all this noise," she said pointing in the direction of the game room. "don't know how you can even think, I woulda been requested a room change from classification," she added. I had heard that statement a thousand times.

"Well, okay", I accepted the invitation. We went to her room on the much quieter center hall. The room was no different from mine except she had pictures of her six children on her night stand and a picture of Jesus on top of her locker-closet. Willie Mae told me about each of her children with such pride in her voice. I could tell that these children were her world. Then she told me that she had a problem with check writing. I didn't probe her for details. Frankly, I didn't want to hear about her case. In prison, I learned that sometimes females voluntarily disclose details of their charges in an effort to get you to talk about yours; especially if you had what they called a "high profile" case which is what I had. To boot, there were times when the person lied about her case, just to get you to reveal your case then she would tell all her friends what you had told her and she'd be the "central attraction" for a few days.

Willie Mae talked endlessly about her children and her charge. I had braced myself for the spill about how much Jesus loved me and how I needed Jesus in my life and of course how Islam was a pagan religion. I thought that Willie Mae was going to preach to me, but she did not. She accepted me without trying to change me or make me conform to what she thought I should be. That fact made me like her all the more.

Unexpectedly she said, "Will you go get me a glass of water?" Thereafter, every time she invited me to her room, before our visit ended, I would have to go to the water fountain for a glass of water for her. That became our personal joke so much so that as time went by, she didn't even have to ask, I knew to get her water before I left her room. When she'd see me reach for her glass, that was the cue that I was about to end my visit by getting the glass of water. I visited Willie Mae often; we talked, shared, and bonded with each other.

I had nurtured a friendship that I had not intended to develop. My plan had been to be a loner. I wanted to be left alone. Although I was civil, polite and courteous to all the other residents, I kept a safe personal distance. Yet here I was with a "friend". There were more to come.

AND MORE CHANGES

"Sherral Kahey, report to your living area, immediately," came the all too familiar page over the p.a. system.

"What do they want now", I signed as I complied with the order and reported to my living area. I was settled into my living area. There wasn't any place they could move me. My job in housekeeping was satisfactory. My job supervisor was pleased with my work, and I had to admit, reluctantly, that I rather enjoyed my job. So why was I being summoned? I walked into the rotunda and to the dorm control center.

"What cha wan', Kahey?" barked Sgt. Addams, the dorm control officer on duty.

"The page said to report to my living area," I answered.

"Well, I ain't paged you and ain't nobody called here fo'ya' so . . ." the phone interrupted her speech.

"Yeah, she here now" said Sgt. Addams into the phone, "okay, she on the way". She hung up the phone saying, "Kahey, they want you in classification."

"Okay, thanks," I said idly. She had already started writing my pass before she cradled the receiver. I knew that this call could only mean that I was being reassigned to another job. I liked my job and was comfortable with it. Comfortable was an enemy to the order of things as far as administration was concerned. Being Comfortable usually meant that one had time to think and analyze things. Institutions such as penal and mental facilities, did not want to contend with having to second guess inmates who had time to think. Their solution to that 'problem' was to medicate inmates. So they pushed psychotropic drugs in the guise of medication. Most of these "medications" turned normal women into zombies. I wanted no parts of the medication. I was neither a pill popper nor a pill pusher.

Pill pushers were comparable to the drug dealers in society. They would get on the psychotropic medication and at medicine call, they would smuggle the drugs by pretending to take them and then sell the drugs to inmates. This was the way many people made extra canteen purchases. Life behind bars paralleled life in society in many uncanny ways. This was called "swinging medication". The person would put the pill or pills in her mouth and then hide it under her tongue or in her jaw, drink water, and then open her mouth for the security officer to check to be sure she swallowed the medication. When the inmate left the medicine area, she would take the pill from her mouth and subsequently sell it to a 'pill junkie'. It was big business in prisons. Many times a person would get her drugs in this manner because she did not want it documented with the parole and pardon boards that she was on psyche medicine. Often when these boards learned that a person was taking psychiatric medication, they would not want to release the person. So they would deny their release. It was better to get the drugs illegally than take the chance of a denial of one's freedom.

Others bought these drugs because they had habits that they enjoyed and wanted to maintain. Some simply wanted to sleep their time away, so they stayed high on drugs. Outside forces had enough control of my life; I surely did not want to relinquish my limited control to drugs.

In classification I was given a job change to the infirmary where I would be the equivalent of an orderly in a hospital. I was one of three infirmary workers. Blanche Ledet was the senior infirmary worker, not in years or age, but had been working in the infirmary longest and was usually the one assigned to train the new workers. Blanche told me that only murderers were assigned to work in the infirmary because other inmates usually had drug or drug-related charges, or they were thieves and shoplifters. Therefore, those types were a risk for working in the infirmary due to their access and exposure to the drugs and other medicinal items. Blanche was a quiet person, but volunteered to tell me that she had killed her husband because she had caught him in bed with the neighbor. The neighbor had testified against Blanche. She got the maximum sentence for Manslaughter which was 21 years. I asked Blanche why she had not killed the neighbor and Blanche matter-of-factly replied, "My beef was with my man not the whore he was dicking down!" Dicking down was yet another prison term, one of many, that meant "*having sex*".

Jessibel Guillot (the first name pronounced like "*Jezebel*" in the Bible) was the other worker. She was a mean-spirited female who did not say much. My instincts led me to construe that Jessibel did not like me. Blanche said that Jessibel didn't like anyone and never got along with other inmates. This was why she was given the job in the infirmary. She was away from people and was not closely supervised. She wasn't rude toward me, but I would catch her glaring at me at times. Other than knowing that Jessibel had committed a murder, I did not know any specifics. I asked Blanche one morning when Blanche seemed to be in one of her rare talkative moods her reply was, "I only talk about my charge. If Jessibel wants you to know, you can ask her and she'll tell you." Blanche did tell me that my predecessor had the same first name that I had. I thought that was a coincidence. It meant that the personnel in the infirmary would not have to remember another inmate's name.

There was nothing special about the job in the infirmary although it was one of a few coveted job assignments. We worked separate shifts that over-lapped. We did get to see each other on the job for a few hours in case there were instructions or information that needed to be passed on or in case there was a need to have more than one worker on hand for various reasons. Blanche had her choice of work hours. She worked from 5:00 a.m.-2:00 p.m. Jessibel worked from 8:00 a.m.-5:00 p.m. 10:00 a.m.-7:00 p.m.

Our job supervisor was a pleasant black woman. She was head nurse and was in charge of the daily routine in the infirmary. Her name was Judith Holt. Ms. Holt was a tall thick black woman. She had a beautiful head of permed, black hair that I thought was made black with the help of Miss Clairol. She was a medium brown; very neat in her white uniform, hosiery and shoes. Her uniform always appeared to be crisply starched and her shoes were so white that they hurt your eyes. She had eyes that were big and beautiful yet sad. They were the eyes of the proverbial deer in the headlights. On days that were slow, she would allow us to get off work early, but we were always "*on call*" for emergencies that may arise. Being on call meant that we were always available for work whenever we were needed.

Inmates came to the infirmary for "sick call" in the mornings from 7a.m. until noon. The infirmary was always full of inmates. Seventy-five per cent of them were trying to get drugs Twenty percent of them wanted to be excused from work. The remaining 5% had the nearly impossible task of trying to convince the nurses that they were indeed ailing. Nurses had been trained and instructed to believe that all the inmates were liars and were trying to con them for drugs or into getting a duty status called a "C". A "C" was the abbreviation for No-Duty. I never understood why it was called a "c". There was also the status "A" which meant that you did not have any restrictions. The "B" restriction was the one for inmates with certain restrictions such as: sit to work; no use of left (or right) hand; must work near a bathroom; no exposure to sun; light duty; work half a day; and there were many others. Usually, if a person couldn't get the "C", they would settle for a "B" duty status that allowed them to do limited work.

"Hey, Girl, don't sweep my feet!" she said. I was at work this particular morning and was spot cleaning the sick call area. There were only three people waiting to be seen. This was because it was so early. Blanche and I had switched hours for the day because she wanted to attend one of her church revivals.

I didn't look up immediately to see the owner of this demand. I was truly fascinated by a set of the smallest feet I had ever seen on an adult. As my eyes trailed upward to meet the eyes of this person, I surely didn't have far to go. The lady was about 4'8' tall. She had a stern look on her face and my first thought was, "S*he has a big woman living inside her*".

"Ma'am, I am not going to sweep your feet", I said politely.

"Better not, that means I'm goin' to jail," she continued. I looked around the room to make sure that this was indeed 'jail'. I wanted to say, "you have arrived!". Instead I said, "Okay."

"You're that Muslim, aren't you?" she asked. Again, I wanted to be sarcastic and say, *"Isn't that obvious with my wearing apparel?"* Instead I simply affirmed her inquiry.

"I'm Lori Verette."

"Who cares," was my thought. I was in a mood that day. Orally, I responded, "you can call me Sherral, nice to meet you."

"I see you all the time. I live on C-center hall." She continued.

Lori Verette was just shy of being a midget. She was a pretty woman, tidily dressed. She had a neat figure, small waist and hips that were too large for her short body. Lori had medium length hair that looked to be permed. The only make-up she wore was red lipstick. She didn't need anything else. Lori was a natural beauty. One could tell that this female had been a "knock-out. She sustained the qualities of a glamorous female.

"Yeah, well get away from me with that broom. I'm superstitious," Lori informed me.

"Okay, I'm finished out here anyway," I commented. It was as well, because the infirmary was becoming busy. Breakfast was over. It was time to scheme a way to get out of work for the day. The infirmary would soon be crowded with those who did not want to do anything except lie in bed pretending to be ill until after working hours; then a miraculous healing took place.

As I was entering my room following my daily tour of duty, someone called out my name. "Sherral", the person called, "hey, I just wanted to apologize for this morning." It was Lori Verette.

"Why?" I asked, not really wanting to know, but that was the polite and expected response.

"Well, I was ugly to you, but really, I'm not a morning person. I do better later in the day or after I have had my coffee." Lori told me.

"No, need to apologize, I didn't take offense, but your apology is accepted." All I wanted to do was get inside my room, close the door and close out the world for a while.

"Well, I didn't want you to think that I am that way all the time, like I'm a witch or something." Lori said.

Why did it matter to her what I thought of her? I didn't even know her and at the moment, I really wanted to get away from her.

Not that she was unpleasant or unkind; I simply wanted to relax from my day of work.

"Lori, I didn't think anymore of the situation, it was really nothing." I wanted to end the encounter.

"Well, I surely did. So, I wanted to ask you to forgive me."

"And I did," I replied in the hope that this would end the conversation.

"I'm glad of that. So what are you doing now?" Lori asked.

"Well, to be perfectly honest with you, I am trying to get in my room and rest from my day at the infirmary." I thought that being blunt would eradicate the issue.

"What's stoppin' you?" Lori inquired.

"You," was my answer.

"Now look who's being rude," Lori asserted. For the briefest moment, we stared at each other, followed by an explosion of laughter. Laughing relieved the tension. I wasn't weary anymore. I felt refreshed, renewed, restored. Laughter is medicinal, even healing. Laughter was rare inside the confines of this prison. When there was laughter, it was done as a mockery of someone or at the expense of another's feelings.

Lori and I were laughing at ourselves, at each other. The laughter also initiated a lasting and rocky friendship for us.

"Okay, I did what I came to do, even got a good laugh out of it," Lori said after the spasm of laughter, I'ma go but I don't see how you can do that with all the noise in this area." Lori pointed to the game room.

"I manage," was my retort.

"Okay, let me go, see ya." Lori said walking away.

I didn't respond. I opened my door and entered my private domain. This was my cocoon. The one place where I could lower the guard; come from behind that wall I built around myself; and take a sigh of relief. I had made it another day. I had survived the inmates and the guards. I avoided lockdown another day; didn't get into any altercations, was not called any ugly names, and no one stared or glared at me. I was no longer the spectacle. I was no longer the weird inmate in the weird clothes. I was "The Muslim". That was the first name that I had been given; although there were other females on the compound who professed to be Islamic. Then I was called the "Muslim Sister". From that nickname, I was called "the sista" and finally the name that carried me throughout my incarceration was simply, "sista". Being nicknamed by the other residents meant that I had been accepted or, acknowledged as a person to be respected. I had no problem with *R-E-S-P-E-C-T.*

MY SISTER

I sat there alone on one of the few benches that were scattered in areas around the compound yard. I did not notice when she had joined me. I sat there with a bag of canteen items that I had gotten as pay for one of the poodles I had sold to another inmate. I was nervous because if the security officer that manned the control thought that I was "smuggling" something into the dormitory, she would call me to the control, ask me to show her what I had and confiscate it. I would get a disciplinary report.

I surely did not want to get the items taken from me; I also didn't want to get any disciplinary action taken against me. I sat on that bench oblivious to anything or anyone.

"You trying to think of a way to get that "ditty-bag" of canteen inside?" came the question that brought me back to the present. I looked round-and-about and there she sat. I did not know where she had come from or how long she had been sitting there. I did not answer her query initially. I did not know this person; so I did not trust this person. I looked at her.

"I am not a confidential informer if that is what you thinking", "she said. Here again were two new prison-vocabulary words. A "ditty-bag is a clothe sack with a draw string closure. It was used to transport items in and out the dormitory. The practice of carrying the ditty bag was not unusual, but the security officer reserved the right to examine the bag if she thought that there was reason to do so. A confidential informer, also called a CI, was a person who was friendly with an officer and would usually provide the officer with information about an inmate who was violating.

"I work in the kitchen," she offered, continuing, she said, "Sometimes people come to me asking me to get food for them to bring you. I'm a cook, so I can come and go in and out the commissary without having to get permission or explain why I was in there". Still, I was speechless. With the information that this person had volunteered, I thought she was going to ask me for some form of payment for her services, which was the way of prison-life.

"My name is Mary, Mary Perrnell. Hell, everybody knows me, you've seen me, huh?"

"I'm Sherral" was all I offered.

"Hell, Sista, everybody knows you", she replied. "I been wanting to meet you, but I am always at work in the kitchen or I am sleep in my room. I came out for some air. I'm off today and been sleep all day long".

Mary was one of the most beautiful black females on the compound. I had seen her several times. She was dark-brown, very close to black. Mary was average height for a woman, but she was top-heavy. Her hair was cut short and she must have used dye on it because it was so black that it looked blue. Her hair was always immaculately combed and styled. She wore eyeliner, foundation and lipstick every day. In fact, I had never seen her without makeup. Mary was classy.

"You trying to think how you can get past that guard with that bag, I know", she said again. I'ma go to the control and talk to the officer, while you get in your gate," she ordered.

"Okay", I was at a loss for words. Mary did exactly what she said. The officer was distracted and opened the inside gate that provided me entrance to my wing. I had gotten in with my food items. I was relieved and at the same time, I was excited that I had been able to get over on the officer, the system. It gave me a rush.

I didn't see Mary again for about a week. When I did see her, I thanked her for helping me.

"Never mind, Sista, that's what we always do when one of us is trying to smuggle stuff in our ditty-bag", she said. Mary had a southern drawl; she spoke slowly, and her voice bordered on a whine. I had observed Mary prior to our meeting and even more so afterward. She was a private person, and I also knew that she bought "medication" which explained why she slept so much and so long. Even in her white kitchen uniform, Mary looked gorgeous. Her white uniform never had stains on it. She wore it starched and ironed. Mary presented the impression of a rich girl, but I knew better. She was doing some serious time so I knew that she did not have money. She just carried herself like the world was hers and she could have it at any time.

"Sista, I like you", she said in a declaration. "You gonna be my "sister cause these 'hoes'll take advantage of you. I can tell you who to trust and who not to trust". That was the beginning of the formation of my prison-family. Mary wanted more than "sista" from me. She wanted me to be like a sister to her. For whatever reason, I did not offer any rebuttal. We were sisters and so it began. *The family*. The prison-life family structure designed to ease some of the hurt, the pain, and the loneliness that accompanied incarceration. Family was a distraction. It was an outlet for what would have normally been the worst of situations. The Family was a bond between inmates that said, "We are connected." Family substituted for the family an inmate left behind. Family was made up of a "husband", wife, children, sisters, "brothers", aunts, "uncles", nieces, "nephews", and even grandparents. Sometimes the family inside the confines of the prison walls was better structured than those in society. There were those who "played" on the value of Family, but in a majority of cases, Family was taken seriously. Family stuck by each other; Family went to lockdown together; Family looked after each other and Family was always there for each other in times of need and crisis. Older females were looked up to and respected as being the "mother" in the family. Mothers typically provided good sound advice to the "children". The children seldom followed the advice, and usually found themselves on lockdown as a result. Family in prisons are basically no different than those in society with the obvious exception that these 'family members are not connected biologically, and the obvious difference that the family members are of the same sex regardless of their sexual orientation.

END OF THE BEGINNING

One year had passed since I stepped foot onto the compound of the Louisiana Correctional Institute for Women. The days seemed endless, but that first year came and went in a flash. Was that a good thing or a bad thing? I did not know. I had completed one year of my life sentence "without the benefit of probation, parole, or suspension of my sentence". I sat on my bunk on the one year anniversary of my incarceration. I reflected on the past, last and first 365 days of my life sentence. I wondered how many years would go by in a flash; how my children and my sister were making their adjustments; was it as challenging for them as it had been for me? How many birthdays and other milestones in my children's lives would I miss? I walked to the long narrow window in my room that looked out onto the immaculately manicured prison grounds. I stood there for several minutes before realizing there were tears streaming down my cheeks.

I did not want to be here, I wanted to be free. I wanted to be with my children, my sister. I wanted the pain to go away. My chest felt as if there was a block of led in my chest cavity instead of my heart. I wanted to cry, to wail, to scream but I knew better than to show such emotions even privately. I didn't want to go take a shower and I didn't want to lie in bed and "face the wall". I covered my mouth with both hands and stifled a screech. The tears continued to fall. The hurt remained. It was a muggy weekend day. People were bustling all over the compound as I looked out the window. I was in a dormitory that housed nearly three hundred females, and several guards nonetheless I felt lonely and alone.

I walked away from the window before anyone saw me; returned to my bunk, and tried to take a nap. The tears had subsided, but my heart was no less heavy. It was then that I had a life-changing revelation. "Sherral", I whispered to myself, "you will lose your mind if you think beyond these walls."

"No", I answered myself, "I will lose my mind if I do not think beyond these walls!" It was during this first year. At this particular point in time that I understood the importance of thinking *beyond* the confines of this facility. I made a promise to myself, lying on that hard bunk, dried tears caking my face. I determined that everything I did from this point forward would be done in preparation for my release. I also decided that I'd get up, go to the phone, and call my sister, and talk to my children.

AFTER THOUGHTS

A ritual I began that first year and consequently maintained throughout my incarceration was—at the end of each year on December 31st as I stood facing the east to pray, as a Muslim and even when I was on my knees praying to Jesus as a Christian, I thanked Allah/God for keeping me in the previous year and I thanked Him for my freedom in the upcoming year. I did that for 28 years without falter or fail.

During my first year of incarceration I learned most of what sustained me throughout my 27 ½ years of incarceration. It was during my first year of incarceration that I met some of the people that would impact my life for all eternity. It was during my first year of incarceration that I began using life's lessons that I had learned prior to my incarceration to help me while I was incarcerated. I learned priceless life lessons behind worthless prison walls.

The truth is no matter where one may be, inside a penal facility, a mental institution, or in society, the people are the same, the circumstances are the same and the results are the same. People behind prison walls are no different than people in society. After all, where did the people in prison come from? People make mistakes. The strong people learn from their mistakes and move forward with their lives taking their lessons with them. The people weak people do not learn from their mistakes and are destined to repeat them.

Life has choices; choices have consequences; consequences affect those we love. We say, "*This is my life. I can do what I please,*

I'm grown!" Yes, it is your life and my life is mine, but the choices we make have a domino effect. The choices I made changed the lives of all the people who loved and cared about me. My choices broke the hearts of those that loved me and wanted a better life for me. My choices brought tears to my loved ones' eyes. I never intended to hurt any of them. My choices caused my loved ones to alter their lives to accommodate my mistakes. My poor choices caused consequences that my family had to endure.

When our choices reach out and touch the lives of others, it is not our life, it is the life we live for the ones we love; the life we live as an example for those who are watching us to see how we will respond to situations. When we make choices for our lives, we don't give a thought to the people that would be pulled into the whirlwind of our choices. It is not a solitary world where we live. Each life touches another's life. Each decision we make is not an individual one but one that causes our loved ones to make or change their decisions. Each mistake is shared by those we love even though we do not intent to hurt or involve them. My beloved auntie used to say that the road to hell was paved with good intentions.

Hindsight is 20/20 vision and in retrospect, there were mistakes, decisions and choices I made that I would not make today. I used the knowledge and understanding I had at that time. Although I would not make the same mistakes, I can honestly say that there are no regrets in my life today. I met people that I would not have met. My life was touched in a life-transforming way by those I encountered. By the same token, God used me to help, encourage, and enlighten the lives of others during my incarceration. I met people that will forever be members of my extended Family and that I love as much as I love my biological family members. I survived the madness that was designed to destroy my mind, body, spirit, and soul. I survived.

Twenty-seven and a half years is a magnanimous chunk from anyone's life. I missed a majority of my children's lives. I cannot take any of those years back. I cannot change what has happened during my incarceration. I cannot ease the pain that my choices caused my family or me. I cannot make up for the "lost" time. Although, the time for me was not lost, I was lost in time. I cannot regain those lost years. They are gone forever.

I can wake up each day thankful that I am not incarcerated. I can thank God that I have been given the change to live a full life and help others to make better choices. I can live for each day, look for the beauty in each day and keep my head up, my thoughts positive, and my direction onward and upward. I can show what God has done in my life. I can believe in the miracle because I am a miracle.

I refuse to live a life where I have to apologize for my past mistakes. I have paid my debt to society. God cancelled my debt. Other than to love my fellow humans, I owe no person. I refuse to have my past mistakes drudged up to defame, belittle, or disgrace me. I will use my mistakes to help others not to make the same ones that I made. I will speak and testify of the goodness of God and I will tell my stories to deter others from the path that chopped more than a quarter of my life away.

Through it all, Jesus had me when I didn't have Him!